#SheWins

Harrowing Stories From Women
Who Survived Domestic Abuse

Alisa Divine

Personal Power Press, Inc.

Bay City, Michigan

#SheWins

Harrowing Stories From Women
Who Survived Domestic Abuse

Library of Congress Catalogue Card Number: 2019931715

ISBN 978-0-9821568-7-2

Printed in the United States of America
Personal Power Press, Inc.
Bay City, MI 48706

Cover Photograph By:
Nikki Closser, www.nikkiclosser.com
Cover Design By:
Parker Haller, parkerhaller72@gmail.com

Disclaimer: The author and publisher have utilized their best efforts
in preparing the information in this book. The stories in this book
have been told to us as each woman's experiences and recollections.

Foreword

In life, we climb, we fall and sometimes we are tossed so violently that we doubt we can survive. And yet, something in us "knows" that we are inherently loved and lovable.

#SheWins both dares us and compels us to travel with our sisters, mothers, and daughters who have experienced the depths of the physical and emotional abuse of domestic violence — that twisted and distorted landscape of a gaping wound where love equals pain. It's a fun house mirror that makes mockery of love and manipulates to survive — for surely we would see such a monster lurking behind that charming face. It is the unpredictable terror of being with one who comes undone, out of control. Love then becomes shame and hiding in isolation. It's sticky and seductive — so compelling to be needed, and to be the one who is necessary to fix the abuser.

To dare to leave, to stand one day and say, "No, no more," is to become bigger than one's fear. It is the first step we take with these incredible women to recover the pieces of themselves that imploded upon that first blow. It's to realize, in part and someday fully, that love never imprisons us, never exploits our goodness, or seeks to decimate our personhood.

#SheWins is when love wins — when that which is within us pulls for a life of meaning, healing and wholeness. We gaze in the mirror beyond what happened to us and are able to see the reflections of our soul, the power that we had all along. And despite our pain, we have become stronger, more compassionate and have burned great purpose into our heart.

Our sisters here tell their compelling stories, and give us their images of before and after. They have lit the victorious path to our freedom. More magnificently, they have opened the possibility for humanity to win. When #SheWins, we all win.

It's your turn. Believe.

Tammy L. Bernier
CEO/Owner, Duperon Corporation

Introduction

Raw Survivor – Survivor of War
(Remarkable Amazing Wonder)

On average, nearly 20 people per minute are physically abused by an intimate partner.

THE IMAGE:
It starts out as the wonder of a garden lovely
With all hope flowers grow and bloom.
THE CAMOUFLAGE
Feelings of security, the perfect unity — solidarity, the dream come true.

THEN
Energy shifts…undefinable when. Reality sets in. Imagine — If you will:

FOR HER: (BAM) First blow…from the love of her life — What happened? Her thought dizzy with shock, oh the humiliation, the disbelief, "how can this be. Oh my God, they said they'd cherish me." Mind spinning, reflecting on yesterday, she's thinking…how, who, when, what did I do then that I deserve this today!

OUTSIDE: She hears the utterance of a few. "She could leave if she wanted to. Why does she stay, so sad," they say. Oh, well, it must not be that bad."

1 in 3 women experience physical violence by an intimate partner.

Alas, the first blow is not to be the last.
This time a kick — a tsunami rumbling in the nucleus of her core, this one knocks her to the floor. The flaming mountain erupting through the fountain…of her blood-stained, swollen lips.
Comes with it, a taste of bitterness.

There is absolute fear here and if we tune closely in her eyes, we see the question she asks at least a dozen times — "Do I stay under a familiar roof to clothe and feed my kids? A reason to stay you see, is to keep them warm and safe."
1–15 children witness Domestic Violence in the home.
Confused, abused, she will do what she has to.

Is it possible that even a disaster area can become a comfort zone?
Perhaps, fear is more gripping stepping out into the unknown.
Domestic Violence is the 3rd leading cause of homelessness.

INSIDE A
Spiritual warfare. Insecurity not yet identified. Intimidation hides the truth of cowardice. It's a blend of antipathy and violence. Doubt commingling with the sweat, the musk of masculine powerless. And, it's being taken out, on she is RAW, she is a survivor, a prisoner of war.

A warzone where retreating is out in the open. Nowhere to escape within the walls constructed with hostility showing signs of brutality. Where hatred is disguised as love. And with every black eye, she having to justify, giving an explanation that'll satisfy those on the outside, because She survives being a prisoner of war.

HOW?
She arms herself with her wounds and pleas, as he strikes out at her with the weapon he pleases. During the unconscionable, she is stronger than she thinks.

As the gun points to her temple, a silent plea is heard within her temple. And this time, still she breathes.

The knife draws from her the liquid of life. Each pound of flesh removed, she survives. Each pound from worry she lose, she survives.
And 19% of Domestic Violence involves a weapon.

ON THE OUTSIDE:
Everything looks so pretty tho – oh, the layers of makeup she uses to hide the raw zone of war.

What happened to the garden lovely??? Each slap in the face, survive she does. Each bruise to her body gone and come, she survives because, each bruise to her heart large enough to cup the vast ocean water. She is a survivor.

Each "Bitch" she's called, emotionally she survives.

Each time she hears, "You walk out that door, I'ma fuck you up" physiologically she survives.

These words spoken, "You ever try to leave me, I'll hunt you, find you and kill your ass," psychologically she survives!
*18.7% of women have experienced threats of physical harm by an intimate partne*r.

Enough. Her Spirit whispers to her Soul. Her Soul whispers to her heart. Her heart whispers to her mind. Going to a place high within, she begins to hear "I am a survivor. I am a survivor."

THEN. Energy shifts…Definable when. Truth's realization sets in. Imagine – If you will:

A choke hold. Her breath wafts across the enemy's face. Eye to eye… Soul to soul…Spirit to Spirit. A force inside, guides her to vocalize, "YOU WILL NOT KILL MY SPIRIT!!!"

In an instant, her presence reveals how brave she is. Layers to his soul she peels, discovering the concealing of an Achilles heel, a psyche of destruction and defeat.
Her Spirit has great tenacity. She believes now it's time to leave — one way or the other. And she prays, that if he preys upon her, does she fight to the end?
1 in 3 female murder victims are killed by intimate partners.
Or, if need be…to save her life, is she willing to take his.
She is Remarkable…She is Amazing…She is a Wonder.

SHE IS RAW

She's out of the zone of war.
A prisoner no more. She looks up to the heavens.
A prisoner no more. She looks down from the heavens.

Beloved IS she.

These words spoken for the Remarkable Amazing Wonder who survives.

These words spoken for the Remarkable Amazing Wonder whose life was lost in this Domestic Violence zone of war.

Author: Anita Caprice

Statistics obtained from NCADV
(National Coalition Against Domestic Violence)

The National Domestic Violence Hotline 1-800-799-SAFE (7233)
Website: DomesticShelters.org

"There is no greater agony than bearing an untold story inside you."

~ Maya Angelou

Amy from Massachusetts

Photographed by Michael Oliver

From Loss To Gain

I wish I could say I was young and naive, but that wasn't the case. I was 38 and a mother to two teenagers that I raised alone since my youngest was 4 months old. I was strong, smart, and independent. And although all of the warning signs were right in my face, I thought I could fix the world with my heart.

We met on a Thursday night for a drink after I had Valentine's Day dinner with my kids. I figured, why not? He was very handsome, extremely charming, and even edgy. He came on strong with an intensity I had never encountered. I felt wanted in a new, exciting way and I was intrigued. He was capable of doing anything — whether it was fixing my light that had been broken for more than a year, doing auto body work on my vehicle, or creating out-of-this-world dinners for us. Once he even showed me how to make a speaker out of a potato! I was pretty impressed. I wasn't looking for love, but I found myself in a fast downward spiral and into a world of shit that I wouldn't wish upon anyone.

After the initial three weeks of spending time with him, he informed me we were getting married that summer. I laughed and said, "I don't even know your middle name." Very sternly he looked at me, and said, "John." I remember getting the chills and now that makes complete sense to me. The following morning he told me he couldn't wait any longer, he just loved me so much. I threw caution to the wind for the first time in my life. I was instantly wrapped up in the excitement of it all and we were married two weeks later.

Once our guests left the wedding, he began to drill into my head that my friends and family who didn't approve of our marriage didn't need to be a part of my life. He said they were just going to try and tear us apart, or they were jealous of him. We had had a lot to drink that day. I remember crying after he threw my "stupid fucking wedding dress" on the floor and kicked it. I also remember praying that if I could just fall asleep, it could all be over. I blamed the "emotional outburst" on the alcohol. Unfortunately, this would soon become a very bad habit of mine.

Throughout the 15 months that we were married, things progressively got worse. I began to dread any time that I would have to be near him. I never knew who he was going to be —"Exuberantly happy and in love with me" guy, or "I hate you, you stupid fucking bitch" guy. Sometimes he was suicidal, "I can't do anything right" guy. I always tried to keep the peace by doing what he asked because it was just easier that way. Slowly and without really knowing it, I had given up control of everything. My only place of comfort was at work.

I remember a Saturday that I came home from a busy day at the salon. I had not been able to answer his texts fast enough to satisfy him. My children were with their father for the weekend. He was waiting for me in the kitchen and grabbed me by the back of my head. He threw me to the floor and started calling me names. Degrading and insanely disturbing things came out of his mouth. He grabbed me again and started pushing me towards the bathroom, insisting I take off all my clothes and kneel in the bathtub. I cried so hard and so loud. I begged and pleaded for him not to make me do that. I had no idea what I was going to endure but the rage on his face told me it was nothing good. As I kneeled inside the cold, hard porcelain tub, sobbing uncontrollably and full of shame, he urinated in my face, and over my entire body. He accused me of having sex with my boss and that's why I wasn't answering his texts. I was forced to continue kneeling through the cold shower to rinse off, supposedly so I would be clean enough for him to rape and beat me repeatedly — because that's what came next.

> *The sexual abuse was so demeaning and degrading, I wanted to die. I hated myself. I made myself sick. I never thought it could get any worse... yet it did.*

One afternoon I found his phone laying in his open hand, lit up on an open screen as if he was using it, yet he was passed out drunk. I picked it up carefully and I could see it was child pornography. Something inside me snapped. I attacked him with his own phone, catching him by surprise. I kept asking him, "What the fuck is wrong with you?" Finally, he said, "I DO FUCKED UP SHIT TO PEOPLE I HATE," and then he kicked me. He kicked me so hard between my legs that I lost every ounce of control that I had over my body.

After some time, when I crawled into my son's room on my stomach,

I was certain I was going to die on my son's bedroom floor. Hours must've gone by before I awoke again. I managed to leave as he was putting fistfuls of pills in his mouth on the couch. I crawled by without a word. A dear friend and my daughter made me go to the police. I will always be thankful for them.

A huge weight was lifted off of my shoulders when the police arrested him. The next morning he was charged with domestic assault and attempted murder. He was unable to get bail. Soon the court dates began — every month, sometimes every week. Fear and anxiety would flare up every single time I learned of a new date. I began to rely on alcohol as my numbing agent. I didn't want to feel that way and I knew I wasn't supposed to feel that way. I was "free" and I should have felt happy, but deep inside I felt quite the opposite. My only escape was the booze.

Luckily, I learned about a few domestic violence Facebook pages and found some brave warrior women I felt strongly connected to because of their stories. One woman in particular stood out to me and I began reading her blog. It was like reading my own life story! I knew I wasn't alone. Now she is MY HERO! After making this amazing connection, I was introduced to more and more women opening up and uniting together as a tribe to support and empower those who endured domestic violence. I happily embraced the new support along with the support of my amazing family.

Ten months after his arrest, he took a plea in District Court. The Superior Court charges took four more years. I began turning to alcohol more often. I thought working out and eating better would be helpful and they were, briefly. Along with my mental health, my physical health started to suffer. I learned I had Endometrial Cancer. I needed a full hysterectomy and I was scared AS FUCK!!!!! I drank more than ever but it ended when I was confronted by one of my best friend's mother. I probably wouldn't be here today without her tough love. I quit drinking six weeks before my hysterectomy. It was hard but slowly I began to feel better, both physically and mentally. I discovered a clarity I never knew existed.

When I was cleared to go back to work and back to the gym, I did. Presently, I am at the best place in life that I have ever been. I am 18 months sober and 16 months cancer free. I have hired a coach and lost over 100 pounds. And I have gained immense muscle and a sense of pride — for the first time. The fall of 2018 was my first body building competition. In the Transformation Division, I was able to share my story and my new body, in front of an auditorium full of spectators. I was awarded a score high enough to compete next summer for overall first place.

I no longer walk with my head in shame. I am proud of me, of what I have overcome. I continue to practice self-care and sobriety. I refuse to accept unhealthy relationships. These are my rules, and this is MY life.

It's ok if you fall down and lose your spark.
Just make sure that when you get back up, you
rise as the whole damn fire.

~ *Colette Werden*

Miranda from Michigan
Photographed by Alisa Divine

Some Things Cannot Be Worked Out

Being in a violent marriage was never my plan. When I walked into my geometry class I saw him. He raced motocross and he knew mechanics. He was a country boy, and he became my high school crush. During my senior year, as I was preparing for college, my brother invited him over to go mudding in our backyard. He asked me out on a date and our relationship began in an amazing way. Flowers every week, a Pandora bracelet with beads sent to my work as a surprise, exciting vacations — I was in love. Soon after, I went to college an hour away but commuted twice a week to see him. I eventually moved in with him and he asked me to marry him. My parents didn't agree. However, I knew we were in love and that was all that mattered.

After the wedding, things changed quickly. He lost his job so I worked two jobs to pay the bills. I did all the chores and cooked dinner. I did everything for him because I loved him. A couple of months later when I checked our savings account it was drained. By that time he was doing stupid things, always looking for the next level of intensity in his life. I felt I had to be responsible for him. We began fighting, lots of screaming and yelling. He often threatened to commit suicide, recklessly pointing his gun at himself or at me. He would run out the door into his truck and leave me wondering if he was ever coming back.

One night after drinking, he put his hands around my neck and choked me, but the next day he was sorry. The fights became more frequent and more violent. He isolated me from my friends and questioned me about everywhere I went. Did I meet guys, did I flirt, and did I cheat on him? I felt like a piece of shit. He threatened to divorce me if I didn't have a baby with him. Then on Valentine's Day, balloons filled the kitchen along with a Victoria's Secret gift certificate and a handwritten card. He knew how to put on a show to make everything look good. Later I found out that while I was at work he was having affairs and spending our money on cocaine. Through it all, I never left because I was taught that divorce was never an option and I could always work it out.

The turning point came when we were on our way home from a Christmas party and began fighting in the truck. He told me he was going to kill himself. He pulled over. I quickly took the gun out of the glove box to throw it out of the truck, but he tackled me over the counsel and we both fell out of the truck. Then the gun went off. I felt excruciating pain, like my arm was completely burning and being crushed. All I could think was "this is it, this is the end." I thought I was going to die. In a panic he called 911 and I was rushed to the hospital. I had surgery and lost some feeling in my hand.

We made up an excuse that it was an accident.

After that incident I knew we were done. I didn't want to be with him anymore and I began to peel myself away from him emotionally. I didn't see his flaws before — I only saw the good times. When I stepped away, I saw the reality. I realized the extent of what happened and divorce was my only option.

Now I get to hang out with my friends again. I have the freedom to go to a movie, or have a drink, all simple things I couldn't do before. I'm finishing up my black belt in Tae Kwon Do because it is something that I always wanted to do. I'm not ready to have kids yet. Instead I'm improving myself first by going to college to be a Mechanical Engineer. I went on a cruise with my mom and it was great not having the burden of someone I had to constantly watch over. I want to travel so much more. My brother and I are into fitness and motocross together. I also have an ultimate dream to become a Monster Energy model. I know I can be anything I want to become. I know my goals and I know my self worth.

If you are lying to friends and family to cover up what happens in your household... it is time to leave. If you wake up in the morning and wonder, "Is this what my relationship should be like?"... it's time. Your life is worth so much more than being abused, being put down to feel like you are the lowest thing on earth, and having another person control your life. I realized there are some things that cannot be worked out and sometimes that is for the best.

*I will not let anyone walk through
my mind with their dirty feet.*

~ Mahatma Gandhi

Lovern from Massachusetts
Photographed by Alisa Divine

I Love My Life Now

After winning two back-to-back beauty pageants in 2010, I chose Domestic Violence Awareness as my platform. At the time it was an easy choice to make, as I was a child witness to it during my first 15 years of life. I was privy to the physical, emotional, and verbal abuse my father delivered to my mother while growing up on the island of Trinidad. Almost weekly attacks on my mother were the norm. My father was strict in the way he raised the five of us siblings. Everyone walked on eggshells in an effort to please him enough so that he would "keep cool". But it was never enough. When he attacked my mother and the police would come, it was frustrating because he never would get arrested. As the educated, breadwinner of the family, he was able to talk his way out of it each time...then again domestic violence was looked upon as a "husband and wife thing" back then and not considered the heinous crime it is now.

As the only sibling who migrated to the United States in 1993 to finish high school, I always said I would not fall prey to the kind of treatment my mother endured. Unfortunately, children who are exposed to violence in the home are more likely to exhibit abusive behavior or become victims. I was no exception and became a victim.

The first physical attack, when my abuser slapped me, was followed with an elaborate apology via numerous voice mails and purple flowers with a touching note. I deduced the incident had to be an isolated behavior because he had never acted like that before and seemed sincere when he said he "would never do it again." I accepted the apology. I believed that the "honeymoon phase" of our relationship — when he was charming and brought me gifts — would return if I could prove to him I loved and forgave him after every attack. After all, he was so sorry, but "I made him do it." I believed I was part of the problem. I believed there were things I could do better to change his behavior.

His reasons for attacking me stemmed from jealousy. If someone looked at me too long or if he perceived I was looking at another man, he deemed that as "inviting attention to myself" or "I wanted to be with that person instead of him." Attacks would follow in the form of verbal assaults, kicking, punching and strangulation.

I hid the physical and emotional pain for two years until I reached my breaking point and sought help for the injuries I sustained during the last attack. After erupting in a jealous rage one night, he beat me from 9 p.m. until 2 a.m. the next morning. He grabbed a knife from the kitchen of my studio apartment, pinned me down and straddled me on my daybed. He held the knife to my throat, pressing it hard enough to let me know he could slit it at any time. The more I pleaded for him to stop, the more enraged he became. At times he would stop to hurl verbal assaults then resume spitting in my face, strangling, punching, and slapping me. When he finally stopped, he laid down in my bed and fell asleep. I felt I had no choice but to lay next to him in fear. I sobbed softly. Soon after, I felt the sharpest pain in my abdomen and upper thigh. I built up enough courage and quietly left the apartment to take a cab to the hospital.

I was diagnosed with rib and upper torso contusions. I lied to the ER doctor and said I fell in the shower after he told me he could get me help based on my injuries. I thought getting "help" meant a women's shelter with big open rooms with many beds and a bunch of strangers. I also didn't want to feel the shame associated with others finding out.

Two weeks went by and I heard nothing from my abuser. He then showed up at my apartment, demanding I let him in. He attempted to break the locks on my door. With my body pressed against the door, I called the police on my cell phone. He left when he heard me talking to the 911 Operator. When the police arrived, they found the wires to my landline had been cut and there were wood shavings on the floor where he tried to gain access to the door. I realized how unsafe I was and finally decided to file for a restraining order.

In the years following, it took a long time to regain my sense of self and learn to love myself again. But not before days, weeks, and months of self-doubt, pity, and depression set in. Why had I let myself fall into this type of relationship? Leaning on my spiritual faith helped as well as friends and family whom I had earlier isolated but still loved me.

It was not until years later during a pageant interview that I tearfully related part of my story. After I explained to the judges why I chose domestic violence as a platform, I realized I was not alone.

17

Amazingly, after the interview, one of the judges disclosed to me she herself was a survivor. After going public with my platform, my family embraced my choice to speak up. My mother and two younger brothers moved to the USA in 1998, while my father remained in Trinidad. He passed away from natural causes in 2002 but his legacy of abuse and the effects of it are something that will remain with us for life.

I believe the more we talk about this issue publicly, the better a victim's chance is of seeking help. I conduct educational workshops at middle schools, high schools, on college campuses and job sites through the non-profit I founded, Love Life Now Foundation, Inc. We raise awareness year-round via local initiatives and connect people with shelters on a national level.

I've appeared on numerous television shows: *CBS This Morning, Huffington Post Live, Security Brief TV, NBC This is New England, WHDH's Urban Update, CBS's Centro, ABC's Cityline,* and *BNN's Common Ground* to help put a spotlight on the issue. Radio programs such as Sirius XM's *Jenny Hutt Live* and WBUR have invited me to share my story and the work I do with the abused women through Love Life Now. I am also a proud wife and mother to two great children.

To learn more visit *www.lovelifenow.org* or email Lovern at info@lovelifenow.org.

A woman's true strength is not measured in how she endures pain but rather how she turns that pain into power.

~ Thomas Haller

Kenda from Washington
Photographed by Michelle Taylor Jones

I Had Enough

My abuse started shortly after I had surgery for an ectopic pregnancy. We were staying at his mom's house while I recovered and as soon as I was able, we moved out and got an apartment. We would get together with our friends, drink beer and play cards after work. My boyfriend didn't want me to work when we were living at his mom's, but when we got our own apartment — he needed me to get a job to help pay our bills. I was excited about that. So I got a job with hours to support me taking my boyfriend to work, bringing him lunch, going to work myself, picking him up from work and taking him home on my lunch break. We had different days off and that's when it started.

I would come home from work and he would be drinking. He began accusing me of trying to get with his friends. He even accused me of sleeping with my manager, so I quit my job and got another one. He said it had to be true because we weren't having sex anymore like we used to. I tried to explain to him that things were different since I began working and having gone through the tubal pregnancy. I was very depressed about losing our baby, while he celebrated the loss. Every night, the drunken accusations flew when I came home from work. He threw me against the wall and choked me. I remember thinking, "If I just love him enough, he'll stop."

One time, we were in the bedroom and he blocked the door so I couldn't get out. He refused to let me leave while he stood there screaming at me. So I went for the window, trying to escape. He grabbed my ankles and yanked me back in, causing me to hit my chin on the windowsill and bust it open. Blood was everywhere. The neighbors called the police and told them they heard screaming.

When the police arrived, I had already cleaned up the blood. They separated us, questioning me in the bedroom and him in the living room. I told the cop we had an argument and that was all. He asked me to roll up my sleeves and show him my arms. My arms were severely bruised. He gave the other cop "the nod" and the other cop had my boyfriend put his hands on the wall and frisked him. He found marijuana in his pocket and immediately cuffed him and took him to jail. They booked him for domestic abuse and possession of 40 grams or less. He was out the next day and came straight home. As soon as he walked through the door, I immediately sat down on the couch and curled up into a ball. He came and sat next to me and asked me if we were over. I started crying and proclaimed my love for him.

It wasn't long before it all started again. We had taken in a homeless 12-year-old boy. I remember my boyfriend walking into the apartment with an already half-empty case of Keystone Ice beer and he was angry. He accused me of sleeping with this boy. When I told him he was out of his mind he grabbed me and threw me against the wall and started choking me. The boy bolted out of the house scared for his life and things went black. When I came to, the apartment was empty and I was there alone. I remember it seemed like it took me forever to get to my feet and I went to the phone and called my parents. My mom answered the phone but when I tried to talk, nothing would come out. Somehow, my mom knew it was me and she yelled to my dad to go to my apartment — I was in trouble. My dad showed up with the cops and knocked on the door. When I opened the door, my dad was standing there with a gun in his hand and said, "Where is he?" I muttered, "I don't know." My dad then asked me if I had had enough yet and was I ready to get out. I told him "yes" and he helped me pack my things and get a new start.

I remember having a difficult time being on my own. I was drinking to be with him, and then I was drinking to be without him. My entire life had revolved around that man for a year and a half, and I had all of that time on my hands. I just didn't know what to do. Eventually, I started working two jobs, making friends, and learning how to live without the drama and the abuse. I fell in love with myself all over again. I swore I would never allow myself to experience anything like that again. I didn't have to drink anymore to get through my days.

Today, I love myself and I respect myself. I live with my son and am happy and successful in my job and in my home. I am attending college to advance my career. I have become a strong and independent woman without needing support from a man, and I refuse to allow abuse of any kind. I try to inspire other women around me to be independent and not dependent on a man, even if they have one in their lives — just in case. That way, if they have a good man, it is a bonus. But if things go wrong, they can still manage on their own.

Above all, be the heroine of your life,
not the victim.

~ Nora Ephron

Adrienne from Georgia
Photographed by Leticia Andrade

New Life From Ashes

Lighting up a room, by walking in. The life of the party. The type of person whose smile is contagious. Someone who makes the world a better place just by being in it. I was that person — before I met him. I always saw the best in others. I would give someone the shirt off my back if I thought they needed it. I walked with confidence. I loved the woman I was. This is important to explain, in order to understand what he attempted to destroy.

The first time I met him I should have run from his crooked smile. There was just something about him. He was the most charming person I had ever met. He had never had a girlfriend or a serious relationship before. That should have been a red flag to me. He knew all the right things to say. I fell hard, and I fell fast. The first six months were amazing. Or so I thought. I didn't know he was sleeping with other women at the same time. We never married, we were engaged for seven years.

I quickly realized that he had this magical ability to blame everything on me and to convince me that it was my fault. Somehow, he could talk his way out of anything. If I confronted him about a lie I caught, that he was texting another woman and asking her if she wanted his body, or when he was supposed to be at work and he was seen elsewhere, he denied it. He would not only convince me it was not true, but he would make me feel crazy for ever believing he could be in the wrong.

The first time he spit in my face something inside of me broke. Sadly, I could see in his eyes that my brokenness excited him. It became one of his favorite things to do and I felt more and more worthless. He was able to convince me I was lucky to have him because no one else would want a worthless failure like me. The verbal and emotional abuse became a daily event. I walked on eggshells trying to keep it to a minimum. Something as simple as the dog spilling water in the kitchen or something happening at work could set him off.

The physical abuse soon escalated. The more he put his hands on me — it seemed the more he felt like a man. I was so scared of him.

I would not fight back because I knew he would kill me. I could tell by the look in his eyes when he wrapped his hands around my neck that he was capable of it. He would watch the life start to leave my eyes as he choked me. Then he let go so I could gasp for air.

Sometimes he would stand there holding a gun and I wondered why he never pulled the trigger. I would be hysterical and then I would just go numb. I would stop feeling. Those were the moments he would bend me over the bed and do whatever he wanted, regardless if I said stop. I wished I could just melt into the bed and disappear. I have never been suicidal, and I have never wanted to die, but there were moments when I believed it would have been easier to be dead. He would threaten that if I ever left him, he would hunt me down and finish me off for good.

I learned how to put on a happy face because I could never let anyone know the truth. I think part of it was the fact that if someone knew, it would make it real. Then I could no longer live in the denial that I called home. I thought if I could be perfect everything would get better. If I could clean the house just right, cook the perfect meal, and make sure not to say anything stupid, it would get better. I was wrong. Nothing I did was ever good enough for him.

The violence continued. When I was about six months pregnant with my oldest, he fractured my ribs and ankle. I had a couple friends take me to the emergency room and I told them my dog knocked me down the stairs. I would "hop" between ERs so that no one would pick up on the abuse. Every time I saw a doctor, they would ask me if I felt safe in my home. I think they could tell what was going on. Every time, I would lie.

When my oldest was 2 years old, he would try to protect me from his dad. I wish I could say that when he stepped in front of me, his father stopped screaming, but that was rarely the case. I will never forget the moment it finally clicked that I needed to find a way out. I got a call in the middle of the night to pick him up from the bar or he was going to be arrested. I loaded my two small children into the car and drove to the bar. He was drunk and most likely high on something too. When I was driving home, he grabbed my phone and tried to throw it out the window. Then he punched me in the face and jerked the wheel, trying to run us off the road. My 3-year-old son started screaming, "Daddy's trying to kill us," over and over. I stopped at his friend's house and let him out of the car.

He was standing in the yard as we pulled away. He was yelling and cursing, shouting that I was the one that did this, not him. I continued driving away. I refused to let him endanger my children. Tears stung my cheek where he had hit me.

My oldest asked me, "Mommy what did you do that made daddy so mad?" I knew we had to find a way out. I did nothing to deserve what his father did to me.

It took time to gain the courage to leave. He kicked the kids and me out like he had done many times before. My mother drove twelve hours through the night to pick us up. He even paid her gas money just so we would be gone. As we were getting ready to leave, he leaned in the car and said to my oldest, "You cannot see daddy anymore because mommy is bad."

I wish I could say it was easy at that point, but for a couple of months I desperately wanted to go back. The abuse was ingrained in me, and my abuser's voice remained in my head long after he was gone. As I was trying to survive the abuse, I started to believe that I could not live without him.

Looking back, I believe the verbal and emotional abuse was worse than the physical. With the physical, the wounds started to heal immediately. The emotional wounds lasted far beyond that and the emotional scars can last forever. Whoever said, "Sticks and stones may break my bones, but words could never hurt me," has never experienced domestic violence and abuse. I know the pain and destruction words can cause.

Now I am aware of the strength I possess and the respect I deserve. I married a man who has been a rock, supporting me in my growth and healing. I have been able to help a few friends get out of abusive relationships, which has led me to discover the passion I have for helping women. It is a dream of mine to create a ministry that will help women in abusive relationships as well as their children. I went to a conference to learn public speaking skills to become more comfortable sharing my story with groups of women. I am determined to use the hell I lived through to help others in all ways that I can.

Now that the ashes have settled, there is more new life. My husband and I recently welcomed another baby boy in 2019.

31

She's been through the darkness of hell, endured the most desolate times, and has been made strong through endurance. Now she walks with the fearlessness of a wolf, the bravery of a lion, and the fierceness of a dragon.

~ Unknown

Nicole from Michigan

Photographed by Alisa Divine

Missing The Red Flags

My abuser was well known in the community. He coached our children's baseball and football teams. On the outside we looked like the perfect family. We had a beautiful house and we both had nice cars and good jobs. We met at Eastern Michigan University. He was the captain of the football team. He seemed like a good person, in the beginning. I didn't know the red flags; the controlling behavior, the jealousy, the put-downs. He wanted to control whom I was with and what I was doing — yet he was able to do whatever he wanted. There were put downs, a strategic way to break down another person's self esteem. Often it was in the form of a joke, followed by, "Oh, I was just kidding!" and the empty promises that "it won't happen again." I believed him when he said he was going to change. After a few years we married and had two children together.

Over time, the emotional abuse exacerbated and the physical abuse began. It started with him pushing me or throwing things at me. From dating to marriage, we were together for 19 years and the last year was the worst. I knew the shift in him occurred when there were no more apologies — he experienced enjoyment in having power and control over me. Enraged when I tried to leave one day, he pulled me back into the house, and with the might of his former-athlete build at 6'4" and 340 pounds, he punched me, choked me and held a gun to my head. He described all the ways he would kill me and kill anyone else who came to my rescue. I lived in fear, too afraid to tell anyone for the next four months because I knew that if I left him I would be in more danger. When I told my own mother, she was shocked, but she believed me. Together we created a calculated plan and I fled with my sons to my sister's house for two weeks while he was served a personal protection order.

I filed for divorce and he made it as difficult financially for me as he possibly could. He transferred credit card debt to me and opened up new cards in my name. He drained the money out of every joint account we had, even with a standing court order stating they were to remain.

As I was packing, I realized he threw away one of each of my shoes and boots — leaving me with only one of each.

The appliances I was allowed to take from the home disappeared, except for the deep freezer, which he unplugged and caused all the contents to spoil. Every time we would get close to an agreement on the divorce settlement, he would fire his attorney and hire another — three different times — it was a way for him to still hold on to me, as if he owned me.

Our divorce was final yet we still had to share custody of the kids. He took every opportunity to make the exchanges as complicated as possible. I would pull up in my car to get the kids and he would drive off with them. He would tell me to meet him at the gas station but not tell me which gas station. It was a game to him.

Even though I didn't tell him where I moved to, he had enough information on me such as my social security number, and he called the electrical company and obtained my address. He began stalking me. On a day we were scheduled to exchange the kids, he brought them to my house, when we were supposed to meet at a mutual drop off point. He came to my door, confrontational, and he threw a cigarette into my face. I called the police and he was arrested for domestic violence. That was the first time.

My son also was a victim. When he was 10, his father assaulted him because he wasn't going to make weight for the football team. My son was hysterical and crying because his father threatened that if he told on him, he would come to our house and beat me with brass knuckles and a baseball bat. He asked my son if he knew what raw hamburger meat looked like and told him that is what my face would look like when he was through with me. When I learned of that I called the police, and they told me there was nothing they could do, it was my word against his. There were 13 calls made to 911 that resulted in only two arrests.

Even still he wasn't satisfied. He continued to harass me, and threatened to come in my home while I was sleeping and slit my throat. That seemed to be his favorite threat, to slit my throat. Other times he threatened to throw acid in my face or disfigure me. I started recording our conversations on a tape recorder. It was two years after our divorce was final and he couldn't move on. He was arrested for aggravated assault in 2011.

Finally I was granted full custody without visitation. But he continued to stalk us. In October of 2012, he owed me $30k in child support and he refused to pay. A hearing was scheduled for November 1 and the threats resumed. He demanded I sign off on the child support or he would kill me. The closer the date got, the more aggressive the threats became. I went to speak with his new parole officer and the plan was to arrest him the next time he reported. Upon doing so, he fought off the officers and was missing for days. During that time, he called me more than 95 times. He repeatedly said that he would kill me if I didn't revoke the child support request. With the help of U.S. Marshalls, he was found five days later. My lethality risk was high.

During the court hearing I read my victim impact statement and afterwards the judge withdrew the plea deal he had previously agreed to. This was a first, a win. I always tell victims to write an impact statement because it does make a difference. He was sentenced to 15 months to 5 years in prison. While he was in jail, he solicited an inmate to kill me for $50k. The inmate passed a polygraph, but the prosecutor refused to cut him a deal and the man refused to testify. That resulted in him still being up for parole. A few days later, two more inmates came forward, saying that my ex was repeatedly bragging that they would see him on the news right after he got released for killing my kids in front of me and then torturing me to death.

Because those inmates came forward, the decision was made to review the parole. Meanwhile, two other inmates came forward to tell of a conversation on the bus between the jail and prison where my ex offered them 50k to kill me. Again in 2017 another inmate came forward stating that my ex-husband was soliciting him to murder me. He agreed to wear a wire but there was too much background noise on the recording and the prosecutor decided that there was not enough evidence to move forward with new charges. I wasn't willing to accept that decision and fought fiercely for my family and ultimately the Attorney General of the State of Michigan decided to take my case and prosecute my ex-husband. Over the course of the past year we've had multiple court dates in three counties and ultimately my ex-husband was convicted and sentenced to 13-35 years in prison.

I now find myself lobbying for change in legislation to protect victims of domestic violence. I present to high school and college students on the red flags of an abusive relationship. I counsel victims and survivors. I speak out by doing interviews with the media and raising awareness by sharing my story on shows like *Inside Evil* with Chris Cuomo. Through my advocacy work I have found healing and empowerment. I strongly believe that through sharing my story, I can raise awareness and prevent others from becoming a victim.

Some women fear the fire
some women simply become it.

~ R.H. Sin

Gabbe from Massachusetts
Photographed by Regina Doody

My Week of Hell

On September 9, 2011, I met my abuser. I didn't see him as the pathetic excuse of a man as I do today. He was 6' 3", with brown hair and brown eyes. He had a fierce, exotic look that I found over-whelmingly attractive. He told me he had a strong bond and love for his family. He had a great sense of humor and came across as very charming. He portrayed himself as very personable and likable to everyone that he met. I had no reason to think otherwise.

I guess I didn't find it odd when he specifically asked if I had ever heard of him or knew of his past. When I hesitantly shook my head no, he immediately opened up to me and told me about an incident involving an ex-girlfriend. At that time he was going to court for it. I should have run out of there and never looked back, but I didn't. I was naive. I saw him as an honest man who had nothing to hide. He easily won me over. Little did I know I was falling into a trap — his trap.

Four months into our relationship, he started serving a yearlong sentence in jail. I stood by faithfully, writing him one to three letters daily, visiting up to two times a week, sending photos to comfort him, and answering his multiple phone calls throughout the day. He promised me only the best, as the sky was the limit for us. He painted a very pretty picture of what our life could be. He talked of a house with a big lawn with a white picket fence, kids and a dog running around. I believed him and started to crave that life. I hoped for a bright future for us.

All that changed June 29, 2013, five months after he was released. For six consecutive days I was held hostage and abused in the most sick, twisted and heinous ways possible, by a man who I believed loved me. He started by accusing me of being unfaithful while he was in jail. He didn't believe that I only wanted him. His verbal abuse quickly escalated into physical abuse. I was hit across my face by the back of his hand numerous times. He wrapped his hands around my throat to strangle me. He pulled me back into his car by my hair and yelled at me that he was sick of my lies. He said he couldn't stand me.

I couldn't imagine it getting worse, but my abuser could. He beat me me with a belt across my backside in the middle of the woods during broad daylight. Then he forcibly injected me with heroin against my will for the majority of the week and even sometimes multiple times a day. Throughout that week I was constantly told, "I'm sick of you and your lies! "You're a whore! You're a slut!" What scared me the most was when he said, "I'm going to bring your body out to Western Massachusetts and no one will find it!" It was clear that he was going to kill me. I thought that was rock bottom, but it wasn't. I was forced to perform inhumane sexual acts on his dog. Afterwards he raped me. The worst part of it all was that he filmed everything to use against me as blackmail. He threatened me every way his sick mind could think of.

As his plan progressed, he attempted to get me to quit my job and move away from my friends and family. He told me we were going to get clean and get jobs. All I could think was who is going to hire two 24 year olds hooked on heroin, living in a hotel? On the sixth day, I went to work. I already had called in sick twice that week. He called me to ask if I had told my boss that I quit yet. It was 3:30 p.m. and she was about to walk out the door. I knew I had to make a move. I hung up quickly and turned to her, "He wants me to quit my job and move away from Cape Cod." It was a holiday weekend and she asked if I could make it through the next few days. I told her "no." When she asked me, "Is it that bad?" I burst into tears and blurted out "Yes!" With her and the owner of the hotel where I worked, we figured out a plan for me to go to the police.

On July 5, 2013 I broke my silence.
I left him to save my life. I left him because I respect myself.

March 12, 2014 the jury found my abuser guilty after a three-day trial. He was sentenced to six years. As I stood up in court and read my impact statement, my legs felt like Jell-O, but I knew I was invincible. After reliving my unbearable week of hell, I knew my story had to be told outside of the courtroom and I chose to go public. Before I knew it, the *Huffington Post*, *ESPN*, and *Crime Watch Daily* featured my story. After connecting with domestic violence organizations around the country, I started to meet other survivors. I attended retreats and joined Facebook groups. My survivor sisters and I share similar experiences along with a bond that's unbreakable.

I was a victim and now I am proud to say I am a strong survivor. I am made up of yesterday's despair, today's hope, and tomorrow's dreams. Through every positive move I have made I am stronger than I was that summer. I am stronger than I was yesterday and will be even stronger tomorrow. Nothing can stop me because he did not win this war. I did. I've remained resilient. I am not what happened to me. I am what I choose to become.

You have escaped the cage. Your wings are stretched out. Now fly.

~ Rumi

Meghna from Maharashtra, India

STOP THE VIOLENCE. STOP THE SILENCE. MEGHNA PANT

I was at his house one evening when he first hit me. We hadn't fought or argued. I was, in fact, quietly studying for an exam. He began by shouting and screaming at me. He pinned me against a corner in the wall and pointed his fingers at me accusatorily. He called me names. He said he would break "my walls". His cheeks turned red and his light eyes, which I loved so much, were squinted in indescribable rage. Then, he spat at me. He was scaring me — who was this man? — so I pushed him away. He punched me. I remember that my skull shook. My glasses flew off the bridge of my nose. Tears welled up in my eyes and my cheeks burnt with a hot acid sensation. No one had ever raised a hand on me before. What was going on?

Then the man I loved grabbed my neck and began to choke me. Again, I pushed him away and told him to stop: was he trying to kill me?

This further enraged him. He dragged me to his bedroom, threw me on the bed and proceeded to choke me again. He punched my arms. He punched my stomach. Then he pulled his hands away, flipped me around and twisted my arm behind my back, lifting me as if trying to break my back. I was then yanked around again and slapped a few times.

My survival instinct told me not to fight back. I went limp.

He continued to shout. I don't remember what he was saying. All I remember was feeling like it was happening to someone else. I became numb. I went into shock.

At some point he let go of me. I ran to the bathroom, locked it, and stayed in there for a good hour or two, weeping, holding myself in disbelief. After all, educated women from good families don't get hit. Do they?

He wept and told me it was a one-time "thing" that "would never happen again." Two days later I failed my exam.

The second time he hit me, four months later, it began with a silly argument. That time too he punched me hard across my face. My skull shook, my cheeks burnt, and my glasses flew across the room. That was the first time I admitted to myself that he had a habit of hitting. If I became submissive, like the last time, he would never stop. I decided not to remain silent. I told his parents, who used to say: "I was like the daughter they never had." They spoke to their son and then told me I deserved it. I shouldn't have provoked him. It was my fault.

This was 11 years ago, when the man I loved, the man I wanted to spend the rest of my life with, hit me and continued to do so for the next five years.

I didn't tell my family or friends about these incidents out of a displaced sense of loyalty. I knew what they would say and I knew I wouldn't like it. Despite everything I didn't want them to hate the man that I loved. Yes, I still loved him. Call it naivety … hope … stupidity … but I did. I was convinced that I was not in an abusive relationship. Why? Because he had told me so. He had told me that violence led women to hospitals. Was I ever sent to the hospital? No! He told me that abuse led to bruises and broken bones. Did I have any of that? No! I believed him because I wanted to. A part of me held on to this misplaced notion that he would see my love and he would change. He would stop hurting me. My love was stronger than our pain.

When a man hits a woman he wounds her physiologically, psychologically, and emotionally. What happened when the man I loved hit me? All my dignity, respect and self-worth went away. It didn't matter how educated I was, how independent I was, how successful I was, how many friends I had, how close I was to my family. I started feeling like there was something fundamentally wrong with me. Why else would a man hit me? You see he told me that I deserved to be hit. I didn't deserve to be loved or to be happy … I was a terrible person … I was dumb … I was stupid … I was an idiot. I could do nothing right. I started believing the things he said about me. I stopped laughing.

I started crying. For months, I cried. I'd walk on the streets, weeping. I'd weep in front of strangers. My friends told me I looked miserable. I was. I'd gone from being a happy person to a terribly sad one. I didn't even want to live anymore.

That's when I found my calling as a writer. Writing helped me put a distance with my reality, while immersing me in life's reality.

It helped me cope with a wound that just wouldn't heal, while healing the wound.

In the time I was with my abuser, I wrote one novel *One & A Half Wife*, and a short story collection *Happy Birthday*, both of which went on to be published and receive critical acclaim, even winning awards.

I finally left my abuser one night in 2012 when I realized that he was a barbarian. I had got my period and he didn't let me access my pads that were in his room. This was a small incident in the history of many incidents, but that moment, which had been many years in the making, finally came to me. It was as if a veil had been lifted. I could no longer lie to myself. I left him. It wasn't easy. I faced new problems and many issues. But none of them matched up to the abuse I had faced with him. He had made me strong enough to deal with anything that life threw my way. I was truly, as song writer David Guetta would say, "bulletproof... I am titanium."

I moved back to India. I continued writing. I published more books. I hosted my own shows. I became a public speaker. I began taking up the cause for abused women in my country. Two years after I left him, I was happy again. Leaving my abuser turned out to be the best decision I ever made in my life.

Then, in 2015, I met my future husband. He is the kindest, sanest and most sensitive man who broke through my wall of hurt and cynicism with generosity and tenderness. I've spent years of beauty, love and wonder with him. Today, we have a beautiful little baby girl. Today, I'm in a healthy and happy relationship with a man who believes in me, values me and respects me. That's utopia — when love finds you in the way that you truly deserve.

It's been more than a decade since I was first hit. I realize that sometimes I still suffer. Yet, every time I read reports of violence against women, I feel like I must gather strength within me to speak out.

I know women go through worse, much worse, yet I wish no woman to go through even a little of what I went through. And if she does, as the increasing rate of physical abuse shows us, she must know that there are many like her and, more importantly, that she has options.

Silence is the real crime against women. To speak of it is hurtful, but to remain silent will hurt us more, because this type of silence has a bully. The bully's name is violence. It has to be stopped. Today. Stop the silence. Stop the violence.

Sometimes I find it difficult to believe that I'm still here. But I am. And, more than anything else, I am laughing again.

You will too.

It took me quite a long time to develop a voice and now that I have it, I am not going to be silent.

~ Madeleine Albright

Kate from Virginia
Photographed by Alisa Divine

Killing Kate Chronicle

TM and I had a whirlwind romance. He was a successful Air Force officer with a master's degree, high security clearances and a stable income. He was a person who skated through most of his life utilizing his good looks. He whitened his teeth, he tanned, he wore designer clothes and he worked out constantly. He was charming, in the sense that he knew how to manipulate people. His house was well furnished and immaculate.

I was a working single mom when I met him. TM wined and dined me, and bought me more jewelry and designer shoes and bags than I could have asked for. The relationship moved quickly — too quickly. He whisked me away on a trip to Mexico soon after we began dating. I was head over heels and I felt happy. I wanted a family.

Six months after we met, TM and I hopped a plane to Vegas to get married. The day after our wedding, when we went to brunch away from the Vegas Strip, he briefly let his mask down. He told me that when his ex-wife left him, he mentally went through the process of how he would kill her. He said it in such a nonchalant way, without any emotion. I actually wondered if he was joking. He wasn't. Later, I would figure out it was a warning. He was telling me not to ever leave him or he would try to kill me. At the time, of course, I didn't want to believe it could be true. We had just gotten married and I was three months pregnant with our son, William.

Our marriage was filled with manipulation and control. In retrospect, I recognize the signs. At the time, I didn't realize I was being abused. I always thought that abuse was when a guy hit you or called you a "bitch," or screamed at you. His covert methods of abuse were difficult to put my finger on. But the signs were all there. I was gradually isolated from my friends and family. I wasn't allowed to be on social media. Male friends? Forget it.

Then there were the guns. TM used his collection to intimidate me. He knew I didn't like them. He would keep them loaded under our bed and clean them in front of me. And let's not forget the lies and shady behavior. Like the time he gave me Ambien without my knowledge.

Or when he told me he was 37 years old when he really was 39. Or when he said he was married once when he really was married three times before me. There was dangerous behavior, too. He took me for rides on his crotch rocket. One time, the last time I ever went on a ride with him, I feared for my life. He was speeding on the highway in excess of 125 mph and I thought I was going to fly off the back. When he stopped I was crying, but he showed no empathy. He told me I was overreacting and he had control of it.

He also thought he could do whatever he wanted without repercussions and he was kind of right. He was AWOL from the military when we moved to Florida. He actually relocated our family from Virginia to Florida on the Air Force's dime, and his command had no idea where their soldier was. He knew he'd get away with it. Sure enough, when I did eventually report him to his command, they handled it "administratively." Nothing happened to him. They retired him with full pension and disability.

After being together for less than three years, the abuse escalated to a physical threat and an attempt to drive off with our son. So I "just left," as abuse victims are always told to do. I filed for divorce. I got a temporary restraining order, defended it multiple times in court, ran out of money and dropped it eight months later, then attempted three more times to get another one. All three times I was denied. Lack of evidence, the judge said, despite pages of emails and texts showing harassment and stalking. TM then attempted to drug William. Child Protective Services got involved and he was limited to supervised visitations. I moved to an undisclosed location. Then he suddenly went quiet.

After 10 days of silence, he showed up unannounced at my apartment.

He'd stalked me and found me. My dad was there and we were inside. TM was pushing against the door to force his way in and we were pushing back to keep him out. Then he shot through the door with a 9mm Beretta. Bullets hit my father and me. TM came inside and shot again. One bullet caused my hand to explode in front of my face, with blood splattering up the wall, and another went through my left breast, missing my heart. My dad took a bullet point blank in his side and another in his arm. All of this happened in front of William, only

4-years-old. I was airlifted to the hospital and lost so much blood that I received a transfusion. I almost died. My dad and I both had surgeries. We have all had a long road to recovery, but we are alive, and we are a strong family. TM received a life sentence without parole. He will die in prison where he belongs.

> **After the shooting I went through a range of emotions.**
> **I questioned if he really meant to kill me.**

I was angry that the court system let me down. I questioned how the relationship got to that point. I couldn't believe that I didn't see it. I felt guilty. What if my dad had died? What if William was caught in the crossfire and was killed? All because I didn't see the signs that I was in an abusive relationship. I was the victim blaming myself.

The physical recovery was grueling. My hand was a claw after the shooting and it took nine months of physical therapy to regain motion again. I lost bone and my hand still doesn't look the same. Half of my hand is numb. But it was the emotional piece that I ignored for too long that has taken the longest to heal. Actually, it's ongoing. Complex Post Traumatic Stress Disorder (PTSD) isn't something you just snap out of or recover from quickly.

At first, I spent all of my energy on my physical healing and on William. That lasted for a couple of years, until I couldn't function at work. It scared me and I knew it was time to work on my mental and emotional well being. I took three months off and went to therapy daily. I began to take my power back. It started with little things, like cutting my blonde hair and dying it dark because TM liked long blonde hair and I wanted anything but that. I went back to my maiden name. I was able to change William's birth certificate to remove his father from it completely and give him my last name. I began to advocate, speak out and share my story. With all of the little wins I achieved, I began to feel I was in control of my life again.

My activism is a big part of what has saved me, given me strength, power — and a voice. Along with my parents and William, I was featured in Brave New Films' documentary, *Making a Killing: Guns, Greed and the NRA*. My story has been featured in the *Washington Post, Rolling Stone, Huffington Post,* and in the award-winning documentary

Finding Jenn's Voice.

I've spoken on the steps of the U.S. Capitol with House Speaker Nancy Pelosi. I've told my story to crowds at rallies and protests. In 2019, my book, *Killing Kate* will be released. It serves as a rallying cry for women to come together, rattle the cages of the systems that are failing us, smash patriarchy and misogyny. Most importantly, it shines a light on the danger signs of potentially violent and abusive relationships, so women are armed with the knowledge they need to avoid these men in the first place.

*I am a woman with thoughts and questions
and shit to say. I say if I'm beautiful.
I say if I'm strong.
You will not determine my story — I will.*

~ Amy Schumer

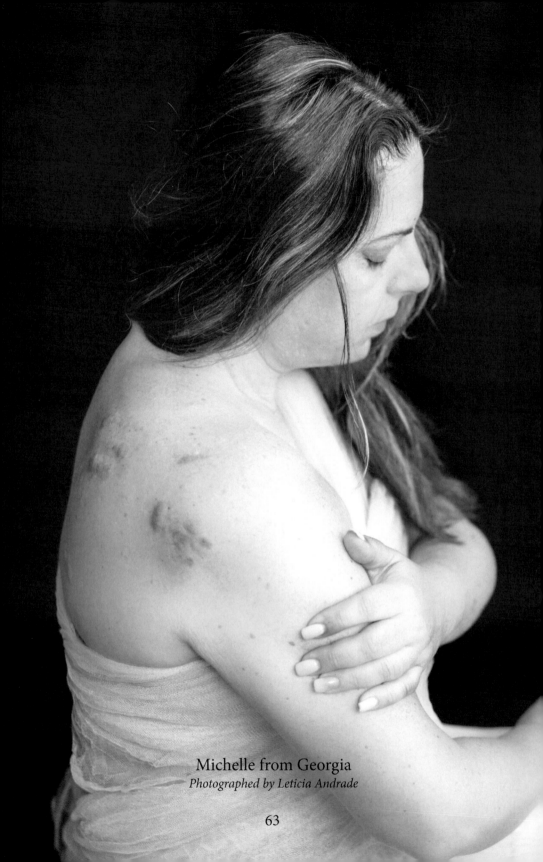

Michelle from Georgia
Photographed by Leticia Andrade

63

Baby Steps

I was sitting on the sofa and started nursing my son. Then I heard "it." I heard his truck. I heard him pulling into the driveway. My daughter ran to the window and looked outside. She yelled "Daddy's home!" Like so many other days, I already had this funny feeling in my stomach. A feeling of dread, worry and anxiety. What mood was he going to be in? Did he have a good day at work? Did he go out with his co-workers before coming home? I never knew.

I could hear the key in the lock and then the door opened. My daughter was playing on the floor and shouted "Hi Daddy!" He acknowledged her and walked into the bedroom. He was cleaning up after work and I heard the shower. I was still nursing my son when I saw my daughter's head peek up. She was looking above and behind me. Her eyes were so big and fearful.

That's when he came charging out of the bedroom. He came from behind and put his arm around my neck. I heard my son screaming. He was in my arms and all I was trying to do was to protect him. My daughter looked so scared sitting on the floor. I tried using my right arm to remove his arm from my neck, while still holding the baby in my left arm. I shouted to my daughter to run to her room. When I broke out of his headlock, the baby was still screaming but I managed to get up holding him with my left arm. I saw the phone lying next to me on the sofa and I grabbed it with my right hand. Cradling my son, I ran into my daughter's room and we locked the door. I sat on her bedroom floor trying to stay calm. I picked up the phone and dialed 911.

Seconds later I heard banging on the door and saw the doorknob move. He was kicking the door. He was hitting the door. The phone was ringing and ringing and no one was picking up. Why was it ringing more than three times, and why was no one answering? I kept looking at the door. I knew it would open. Why was the phone still ringing? I looked at my daughter. She seemed scared and fragile. The baby was still screaming.

Then the door swung open. My daughter's head turned towards the door as he came charging at me. I looked into my daughter's eyes and told her to run to the neighbor and get help. She ran out of her room but he went after her. I panicked. I got off the floor still holding the baby and ran after them. I saw her trying to turn the doorknob but the child lock was covering it. She turned to look at me and he was charging towards her. He tried stopping her. He put his arm around her and put his other hand over hers, holding her back. Then he saw me heading towards the back door and looked confused. He stepped away from my daughter not knowing what to do. He let her go and my daughter managed to open the front door and run across the front yard. He turned and came running towards me. I was still holding the baby, and he was trying to stop me from escaping through the back door. All I could think was he couldn't hurt my daughter anymore. She got away. I was just hoping help was on the way. With the baby still crying, I heard voices approaching the house and it was the neighbor.

In that moment, I knew I needed to leave him. The fear in my daughter's eyes will haunt me forever and the cries of my son I will never forget. We were lucky that day. Maybe we wouldn't be lucky next time.

It wasn't about me anymore — it was about my children and keeping them safe.

After that I was so scared for myself and my children. I took care of them 24/7. I had no family around and I knew I needed to find a job. I needed to provide for my children. He threatened me that I would never have anything. He threatened me, telling me he would take the car away. But I knew we would be free. We wouldn't have to worry about how he would behave every day.

I struggled at first. I moved an hour away closer to my mother so she could help me with my children. Then I ended up getting my own place. I felt safe for the first time but I never let down my guard. Each time our lives felt peaceful and happy, something would happen again. Harassing phone calls. Waking up to hundreds of text messages from him. My daughter telling me she saw her father's car nearby. I always told her it was a car that looked just like his and many people have one like it. But it was him. He would follow us around. He would drive by our house. Even though I had a security system in our house, I never felt safe.

One morning I stayed home and my mother came by to pick up my daughter and take her to school. Two to three minutes after my mother left, I heard a noise at the back door. I started walking towards the door and looked out the window — it was not my mother, it was him! He was trying to break in my back door. Then I saw there was a police officer with him. He had convinced the officer that he lived in my house. Afterwards, my neighbors told me they saw my ex coming and going from my house for months, assuming he lived with me. I discovered he was hiding in my attic.

After that day everything changed. I was not scared of him anymore, I was angry! I became a fighter for myself and for my children. I filed an order of protection to fight back. He was not going to hurt me and he was definitely not going to hurt my children. I did not want them to live in constant fear like I did.

I now know how much strength and will power I have in me. I know what is right and what is wrong. I know what is okay and not okay. I never left him, because I was afraid. I believed I could not do it. I believed him when he said I could not make it on my own. But I did!

Nevertheless, I still look in my rear view mirror. I always check to see if someone is following me. When I'm walking, I constantly look over my shoulder. I do not think that will ever change.

My life is so much better. I remember to take baby steps to get through the day. I focus on how blessed I am. I have two, beautiful and smart children. I feel safe and secure with my husband of five years. Helping others and seeing my family happy, gives me great satisfaction.

*Speak your truth so that others can find the
courage to speak their own.
Share your stories so that others can bond
through sharing their own.
Love yourself so that others can discover how to
love themselves.
Free yourself so that others can learn the tools
to free themselves.
If you want to save the world, start by saving yourself.
The world will learn through your example.*

~ Emily Maroutian

Kim from Australia
Photographed by Mellissa Baker

The Healing Power of Horses

I was in my early thirties, with a career in children's publishing as the product development manager for Scholastic Australia. I was a confident, fit and happy woman returning to our head office after a successful industry trade fair, feeling proud with the outcomes I had secured for the company. Life was good. No, life was great.

Feeling hungry, I headed to our local café to grab lunch. As I walked up to the counter, scanning the blackboard menu, a handsome man stood in front of me, waiting for my order. I was a bit taken aback by his confident essence, complimented by his chiseled looks, sparkling blue eyes and tantalising smile. I smiled back and asked for a salad sandwich. He effortlessly struck up a chat, making me laugh. Before I knew it, we were exchanging phone numbers. I remember feeling butterflies in my stomach as he handed me my lunch.

We started dating. He was the perfect partner. Many times, I marveled: "Wow this man is too good to be true!" I felt happy and safe with him. Finally, I invited him to my home for dinner and importantly, to meet my best friend, Maggie, my rescue dog. Quickly, he moved in and soon we were taking Maggie for her daily walks down to the beach. But over time, something in him and our relationship changed.

A male friend from primary school phoned thinking it would be great to catch up for a coffee or quick beer. My partner grabbed the phone and started yelling at him, my friend hung up.

"Have you fucked him? I know you have." Over and over the same questions and accusations were thrown at me, wearing me down, grinding, exhausting.

"You're lying, like all females, you're just a slut! I don't believe you!" he yelled.

The next minute he slammed down a pen and piece of paper on the dining table.

"Draw your friend's penis! You know what size and shape it is," he demanded.

Rage boiled in his eyes.

I laughed in shock at how crazy the situation was. Incandescent with anger he slammed me against the wall and put his hand to my throat, I felt him tighten his hold around my neck.

"This is no laughing matter," he said through gritted teeth.

Survival mode kicked in. Fighting back the tears, I agreed never to speak or see my friend ever again.

We began arguing more often, over silly things. At first, he would just verbally abuse me — humiliating, frightening, the language of ownership. As time went on, he could no longer contain the need to physically, sexually and emotionally abuse and control me completely. Day by day my self-belief, self-esteem and ability to make my own decisions were eaten away. Like a cancer, his abuse spread, engulfing every essence of my being. My job, and my darling Maggie, were the only comforting lights I experienced during the darkest times.

After three months, something snapped in me and I drew on every calm bone in my body to tell him I wanted to end our relationship. I was surprised when he took the news well and we agreed I would take him to the train station the next morning.

I dropped him off, he said goodbye with the dancing eyes of the charming man I'd first met. I felt relieved to be rid of the monster.

I arrived home after work — so happy it was just Maggie and me. Suddenly, I heard a noise coming from the spare bedroom upstairs. I went up to investigate and was confronted by him.

"What the fuck are you doing here, you were meant to leave!" I shouted.

He replied easily that the mate he was going to stay with wouldn't be back until the next day, could he stay another night?

I gave in and told him he could sleep upstairs in the spare room.

At around 1 a.m. I was woken by him standing next to my bed. He demanded that we have sex and I refused. Thankfully, he walked out of my room, but I had no idea of the perverse mind I was about to face.

The next morning, he told me he would take Maggie for her walk because he would miss her when he left. It was an exciting day — we were about to enter negotiations for the publishing rights to Pokémon. During the talks I received a message from him saying I needed to come home because Maggie was missing. Distraught, I left the meeting. He helped me search for days, but my beloved Maggie was gone. I was now vulnerable again and he managed to work his way back into my life, continuing to stay with me. Several days later another intense argument began. Then suddenly he spat out: "You'll never see Maggie again because you loved her more than me."

He had thrown her off the cliffs to her death.

The abuse became more intense. I knew I had to escape. It was only a matter of time before he killed me, or I killed him in order to survive. I genuinely believed my only other choice was suicide. I slashed my wrists in front of him, blood streamed out. He wouldn't take me to hospital. Instead he bandaged me tightly, speaking softly: "You slipped with the knife, don't worry, I'm here to take care of you."

He kept me under house arrest, cut off from family and friends, no longer in possession of my bank accounts, medical cards, even my contraceptive pills — he controlled everything. Not long after this he made real attempts on my life, the worst when he tried to suffocate me with a pillow.

Unbeknown to me, help was coming. My family was making plans to rescue me. My brother arrived unexpectedly to take me out for a coffee. Instead we went to the police station. As we approached the counter, my brother said we wanted to press charges against my partner for abuse. At first the police were like: "Oh great, another D.V. case." But when my partner's name was mentioned instantly everything changed. It was only then I learned of his extensive criminal background.

I started seeing a psychologist who made it clear. I had been groomed and indoctrinated by my partner. I no longer knew right from wrong

— I had lost the ability to think for myself. But I was determined not to be the victim. I was not going to let him win.

I found a miracle survival tool, rekindling my childhood passion for horses. I bonded with a horse named Sahara. She seemed to sense what I needed, nuzzling my neck, her gentle, warm breathe calming me. More reassuring than words, she began my journey reclaiming my life. It is Sahara I credit with my ability to truly start my recovery. I realized that horses kept my thought processes in the present and that nothing else mattered.

Gentle Transitions (GT) was born. At Gentle Transitions we believe everyone deserves an equal chance to pursue a successful life. With the help of our horses, we are able to encourage each individual to rediscover their inner wisdom. It was time for Australia to wake up to the healing power of horses. It was time to ensure equine assisted therapy and learning programmes were there for the people who needed them most.

Doing what I loved, following my passions and dreams, I was truly happy. He had taken everything, my bank accounts, my credit cards, and my career. But despite the huge financial challenge of building a new life in a new place, I felt strong. It was during that time I was approached by a major newspaper. They asked if I would tell my story, as a survivor of domestic violence. It was to be based around "The most dangerous time of my life."

That first article went viral and created countless conversations about this issue. Even today I still receive random emails and messages from women who read it saying: "Thank you for inspiring me, for making me feel I'm not alone."

I'm comfortable with my past — I'm at peace. Thanks to my horses, an alternative therapist, an amazing kinesiologist and a vivid meditation, my chakras are cleansed, meridians balanced, and energy flowing.

He has recently been released on parole. I continue to tell my survival story when it's necessary. When asked why, my answer is simple: "If my speaking out can save another woman… it's worth it."

The most beautiful people we have known
are those who have known defeat, known suffering,
known struggle, known loss,
and have found their way out of the depths.
These persons have an appreciation, a sensitivity,
and an understanding of life
that fills them with compassion,
gentleness, and a deep loving concern.
Beautiful people do not just happen.

~ Elizabeth Kubler-Ross

Kayla from South Carolina
Photographed by Rachel Thompson-Moore

A Ghost In The Mirror

As a young girl I grew up in a single-parent home with my mother. It was not broken — it was independent. My mother knew she didn't need a man to survive, so I knew that I didn't either.

It was not until I finished my junior year in high school that I first took interest in a serious relationship. I fell head over heels for a boy that was several years older than me. I thought he was more gentle and mature.

Turned out I was completely wrong.

Our relationship was rocky from the start, but since it was my first relationship, I thought rockiness was normal. Being in a single parent home, I didn't exactly know what "love" looked like. So I knew I needed to create my own definition and reality of what "love" was.

The pain started with the words "I cheated" and ended with scars stitched with a horrific story. When things went wrong, I found myself to blame. I thought I needed to fix myself and be better for him.

I survived eleven months filled with threats, isolation, manipulation, belittling and black eyes. I can't say that all the times spent together were bad, but the bad times began to override the little moments of joy.

The worst part of it — was losing myself. I had no idea who I was anymore. I used to be a strong-minded girl who would never lose herself for someone else, but there I was, a stranger in my own skin. I found myself as a ghost in the mirror.

Although I knew times were rough, I hardly knew anything about domestic abuse or dating violence. For sure, I couldn't have been one to fall through the cracks and land in the hands of an abuser. But it just so happened that I was a statistic of one in four.

One day I was feeling happy and safe in my relationship. Next thing I knew I'd been cheated on and was being begged for forgiveness, because he was "just drunk" and didn't mean to. I gave in, but what came after forgiving? He pushed to the next extreme...

That extreme turned out to be a black eye, and a busted nose and lip. But what did he do? Once again he begged and cried for forgiveness. He didn't want to get in trouble and swore he didn't mean to...but he knew what he was doing. Yet I gave in, once again.

I agreed to make up a lie saying that it was someone else and I swore to him I wouldn't tell the truth — so no one thought badly of him.

Did it get better? No, it would never get better.
I was continuously pushed past the limits
and I was afraid to get out.

What happened when I finally gained the courage to get out? Another black eye.

He begged and begged again and at that point I was afraid, once again. So I stuck it out for a bit longer... I was pushed much further until finally, I broke. And I KNEW I needed out.

I cut ties and he burned bridges. What was next? Blocking? No trespassing? Or even a restraining order? Would those really help someone who couldn't take rejection? Someone who couldn't accept the fact that he lost complete control over me?

The answer is no. Matters only got worse.

A month went by. I thought it all may have simmered down and I checked in to see if there was anything of his that he wanted back before I tossed it all out. I got the understanding that he'd changed and things were better with him. He got over being mad and he wanted to see me because he was "going into the Navy."

I wanted to give him the chance to prove it, to make his wrongs—right. So I agreed to give him the opportunity to redeem himself to be a better person, and I believed that he was sorry. But people like that don't change. They just know how to work you and manipulate you.

He tried to kiss me. I wasn't there to get back together with him. I refused his kiss and backed up only to feel him latch onto me. I felt my lip tear about half way. Then I started screaming at the top of my lungs for help and out of fear for my life. Then he yanked me out of my own car, slammed the door in my face and took off. He ran away from what he just had done. I was rushed into plastic surgery... missing 85% of my lip.

All because he couldn't stand seeing me happy without him.

The physical scars hurt and I promise you that the internal scars hurt much worse. But today I am channeling my pain into positivity. I refuse to sit back and let that defeat me. I have started a Facebook page called *Rise Above* to help others become aware of the early signs of domestic abuse. I will do anything in my power to save the next person from what I went through. Love shouldn't end in tragedy but in my case it did.

Now I want to use my story to show that there is life after tragedy.

I am finally free and have been able to find myself once again. I have a passion for something I once knew nothing about, and for that I am thankful. I know that my pain had a purpose behind it. I can stand tall and turn that purpose into another potential-victim's saving grace.

She has been feeling it for a while now,
that sense of awakening.
There is a gentle rage simmering inside her,
and it is getting stronger by the day.
She will hold it close to her, she will nurture it
and let it grow. She won't let anyone take it
away from her. It is her rocket fuel
and finally, she is going places.
She can feel it down to her very core —
this is her time.
She will not only climb mountains,
she will move them too.

~ Lang Leav

Ann from California
Photographed by Alisa Divine

Domestic Terrorism

We were both Scandinavian and our friends thought we would get along well together. In the beginning we did. We had similar thought processes and we were raised with similar upbringings. Looking back, I wasn't in the right mind to make a decision on whether he was the right person for me or not. I was fresh out of my first marriage with two teenagers. When I look back, there were warning signs. He was possessive, jealous, and controlling. I felt like a 5-year-old asking for money — he had full financial control.

After we had a son together, it became worse. He wasn't the center of attention anymore. That is when the Dr. Jekyll and Mr. Hyde personality came out. I never knew who was going to walk through the door. I was walking on eggshells constantly. I knew something was wrong, it wasn't just me, it was him. One time my husband was screaming and yelling at me, and our son, who was 6 years old at the time, hid behind my back and said, "Don't listen to him, Mom."

We moved to Sweden for a year to get his business in Europe off the ground. I hoped the move would be helpful, but our marriage quickly declined. Eventually he took off on a first-class flight back to San Diego, leaving my son and me financially cut off completely. I don't think he wanted a divorce. I think it was another attempt to scare me. There's a saying, that you can only beat a dog for so long before the dog starts to fight back. So I began to fight back. I got stronger. I took back my power. My first husband paid for plane tickets for my son and me to go back to the U.S. When I arrived at the airport, I was served with divorce papers straight out of customs, which he had filed on my birthday.

Until our divorce was final, we were co-living in the marital home. He had put locks on the master bedroom and some other rooms in the house that I had no access to, and I took over a guest bedroom. On one particular morning, he was following me around, trying to start an argument. There was a crazy look in his eyes, which he got every now and then and he was pacing. "You fucking bitch, I'm going to have you deported! Our son and I don't need you," he screamed at me. I went into my room to close the door and he put his hand up on the door frame to stop me. There was a Taser in the room, which he had purchased for me a couple years earlier as a safety precaution when I walked the dog. I picked up the Taser and pointed it at him and said, "Get the fuck out of my room." And he did.

If I had known what was going to happen next, I would have used the Taser to at least have a piece of satisfaction. He called the cops and told them I was threatening him with a Taser. They arrived and took us to separate areas of the house. I told the police that he'd been verbally and mentally abusing me. I was financially cut off and was a prisoner in my own house. But the crazy look I saw in his eyes and the intimidation I felt were not enough. Since he didn't physically assault me or threaten to kill me — I got arrested! I was a stay-at-home house-wife but spent 13 hours in the jail with crack addicts and prostitutes.

I moved out with $5k, no job and no place to live. I slept on couches of friends' houses, until I could get in front of a judge to receive financial support. That was the beginning of a new hell with attorneys, financial ruin, and homelessness. He attempted to prove a case that I was unstable because I pointed a Taser, and therefore an unfit mother. He knew the only thing that would hurt me was going after our son. Because I didn't have a job, or a house, the family court gave him 80 percent custody. To this day, I've spent $100k in attorney fees. My son and I could've had a nice home for that.

During this time I was not only broke, I was broken.

If it weren't for my kids, I probably would've committed suicide. I picked up my son from school and he said, "Mom, let's go home," then followed with, "oh wait, we don't have a home." I just cried. This was his son too. There was enough money for all of us to be comfortable, but this was a punishment directed at me for leaving him. And our son was punished too.

Several months ago my son and I were talking about that period of time, and he said, "Do you remember when we slept in the car?" I replied, "No." And he went on, "Yeah mom, when we didn't have a place to stay for a couple of nights and you parked the car in front of a church and we slept there." I didn't remember. Our minds are powerful. They allow us to forget things that we would rather not recall. Looking back though, I was in survival mode.

To charge forward and continue custody with my son, I found a job with a catering company and rented a 10x10 room in someone's house. Eventually, his father's poor parenting record added up. I gathered enough evidence to be awarded more custody. Then I found a job with a boudoir photography business that was looking for a photographer. I had training in photography and I also found it therapeutic. Sometimes I put down the camera to be a therapist rather than a photographer. And sometimes I was more in therapy than I was a photographer. I loved connecting with women. I helped to build that business until I eventually started my own studio in my home. I found Sue Bryce, an international portrait photographer, took her workshop in 2015 and followed her business model. I was chosen to assist her with future workshops. She also came to my house to tape a video segment and tour of my home studio for her worldwide education site.

I was a single mom who built my business from the ground up.

Sue showcased me as an example to tens of thousands of people on her education site. I've set goals, I've followed through and I've worked hard. Once I started feeling comfortable talking about my domestic abuse experience, I began posting about it in Sue's online groups. Women reached out to me with private messages saying they were inspired by me and my story. They felt like they could stand up for themselves after hearing that I did. The more I talked about what happened to me, the more I felt healed. Knowing I inspired others pushed me forward.

I started the I Shine Project. I work with women who have survived domestic abuse. I invite each woman into my photography studio and I document her story. We celebrate with a gathering of women and view the finished documentary with hors d'oeuvres and champagne. We then raise money for another woman to experience the I Shine Project — to be pampered, to tell her story and to receive her printed photographs in a keepsake box. The women experience powerful support from each other, feel validated and get back in touch with the essence of who they really are — not what's been done to them. It has helped me heal by giving back to other woman recovering.

I would love to see this project grow among photographers across the country and even the world. I want to remind women that even though they've been through a lot, the essence of who they are is still there.

One morning she woke up different.
Done with trying to figure out who was with her,
against her, or walking down the middle
because they didn't have the guts to pick a side.
She was done with anything that
didn't bring her peace.
She realized that opinions were a dime a dozen,
validations were for parking,
and loyalty isn't a word but a lifestyle.
This day her life changed.
Not because of a man, or a job... life is way too
short to leave the key to your happiness
in someone else's pocket.

~ Unknown

Alejandra from Arizona
Photographed by Karianne Munstedt

The Gift of Losing

The extravagant gifts and surprise romantic gestures only lasted a few months. The darkness behind his actions soon manifested into escalated arguments, threatening behavior and vulgar screams hurled my way. Ironically, he said he needed my help. He claimed that his outbursts were a result of a troubled upbringing where he was left to deal with abandonment issues. Only I could help him overcome that obstacle. Maybe I did love him, or maybe my "love" was the deep burden of feeling responsible for saving him. Either way, I needed to help him.

My terror heightened once he purchased a handgun. He began to use it as a way to manipulate our relationship. He pulled out the gun on several occasions and he'd point it to his head to end an argument — me crying in desperation that I would make everything all right. During one drunken night I faced my dark reality when he nearly choked me. Then he kicked me as I curled into a ball on the floor, my head hitting against a wall again and again. I was certain I would not make it out alive. I wondered how my parents would be given the news that their only daughter had died that night. As a reprieve, if you will, it ended with him holding his gun to his head, again pleading for forgiveness.

What was I supposed to do? I could not share my life, my family or my love with someone who had violated my basic human rights, but I was scared. It took more than a week for me to leave him, and I did exactly what victims of abuse are told to do. I never spoke to him again, filed police reports, pressed charges, obtained a restraining order, moved out with a police escort by my side, and reported each phone call I got from him. I thought that was the end and I was finally free.

In reality, my journey had just begun. Going through the legal process of reporting domestic violence in addition to healing from it, proved to be the most challenging chapter of my life. I found my-self diving into books, blogs and videos that taught me about DV. Learning terms like "gas lighting" helped me understand what I had gone through. As I gained knowledge, I became empowered. I cleaned my life by removing people who did not believe me or did not contribute positively. I saw a therapist and stayed in touch with my advocate who helped me through the legal process of pressing charges.

Not surprisingly, I had good days and I had bad days where I would question my own sanity because healing often times felt like I was trying to crawl out of a deep, confusing and dark hole. Sometimes the smallest things were the most difficult to do — listening to a song on the radio or meeting up with a friend. But I promised myself there was no way I was going to let HIM ruin my gift to be alive. I made a decision to work hard, love myself and create the life I wanted.

Then I went to trial for the charges I pressed. No amount of evidence, pictures or witnesses were enough for the jury of six who delivered a verdict on my 27th birthday. My abuser was found NOT guilty!

This is why women don't come forward — nobody believes them.

I kept thinking in between cries of disbelief. I did everything "right" for…this?   I felt defeated by the long, confusing and disjointed year-long court process.

Then my dad said something to me that changed my perspective. "You aren't going to let what's on a piece of paper determine the value of the rest of your life, are you?" His words were like light shining through the cracks in my heart — a beautiful mosaic heart made up of pieces that represented breakthrough moments of my healing. With his words and the support of the close friends and family that held me with their love, I left the courtroom with the most precious gift of all. I learned I was unbreakable. I learned that no matter how many rocks got thrown my way, no matter what a piece of paper said, I won. I have what I wanted — a heart that is free and at peace.

I faced up to the man that beat me after a year's work of self-love, healing and empowerment. I promised myself that I would be a resource for other women so they never have to feel alone, especially when they are facing abuse. I shifted my career to work for organizations that help communities affected by abuse. Now I speak up about this issue and am on a mission to create safe spaces for other victims to heal. I know I won this battle long ago because the enemy doesn't stand a chance when the victim decides to survive. I stand tall and proud of whom I have become.

One day, in retrospect, the years of struggle will strike you as the most beautiful.

~ Sigmund Freud

Megan from Michigan
Photographed by Alisa Divine

Badass Woman

We met during my freshman year of high school. I was a varsity cheerleader and he was a basketball player. I always thought he was cute — there was just something about him. Then a few years went by. When I was 20, I already had a one-year old baby and a failed marriage. You could say that I wasn't very good at choosing men. Our relationship began when he wished me a "Happy Birthday" on Facebook. I hadn't heard from him in years, but I messaged him and we started seeing each other.

For the first couple of years it was a normal relationship. We loved each other and he took on the role of being a father to my son. However, we would get in terrible fights, mainly over him talking to other women romantically. He'd become defensive and would turn it around on me every time. One month after we got engaged was the first time I ever saw his scary side. I was loading the dishwasher and he didn't like the way I did it. He was so mad that he punched six holes into one of our interior doors while screaming at me in front of our son. We began to fight more often. He would call me ugly or fat, but then added he was "just kidding." In his mind, that made the criticisms okay. Once he showed me pictures of girls he slept with and they all were beautiful. Then he asked me if I wanted to see a picture of an ugly girl he slept with. He showed me a picture of myself. I never felt good enough. I felt that if I looked better, he wouldn't be so angry. So I lost 60 pounds but it didn't help.

Everyday, he went through my phone and computer. He said he hated me and called me a "bitch", "whore" and "cunt." Once he woke our 6 year old up in the middle of the night to tell him that his mommy was going to kill herself. He locked me outside of our house in the Michigan winter without a coat or shoes. He tried to kidnap our 4-week-old baby and drive him around when he was drunk. He put me in a headlock and suffocated me until I blacked out. He controlled what I wore and wouldn't let me wear anything he thought was even the least revealing. I felt guilty, even when he wasn't around. The continuous question in my head was, "If I do this…will he get mad?" I felt discouraged from following my dreams. I lived in fear. I was walking in his shadow. I wasn't Megan anymore I was only his wife.

The list of violent acts continued. He threw a lamp at my head. He crashed my car into the tree of our front yard on purpose. When we got into a screaming match, he grabbed me by the throat and pinned me against the stairs. He was looking into my eyes as he choked me. He let go right before I lost consciousness. There were several of these incidences and pushing or choking were his preferred methods of abuse. Once or twice a month he would get so angry with me he'd start punching holes into the walls and doors, breaking glass, or anything else that was around. The second time the same police officer answered my call for help, he took pictures of my bruises, the broken glass and the holes in the walls. He asked me if I wanted to press charges and told me, "Megan, I come to these calls a lot. And I'm really worried the next time I come you are going to be dead." I'll never forget the egotistical smile on my husband's face as they took him away in handcuffs. I pressed charges and he went to jail.

I *know this may sound crazy but I missed him sometimes, I missed the good times.*

For a while, my son asked me if daddy could come home and I had to tell him "no." I found out that being a single parent is exhausting, expensive, stressful, and sometimes I would lay in bed and cry. But at the end of the day, I was grateful. I was alive, my kids were alive and healthy, and I was finally free to be me.

My life is so different now. I started going to church and joined a mom's group. I've made many new friends and go out once a month wearing whatever outfit I want. My career is advancing. I began my own business, Thrive Social. I am an active member of the community, serve on various boards and spend time in volunteer work. I choose if I want to paint my house, buy a dress or get my hair cut. I am raising two kids by myself with my values. I feel worthy enough for the first time in my life.

In the end, I got the kids, the house, and the 401k. He got an 11-year felony for strangulation. Thank you for making me the strongest, badass woman I know.

I am proud of the woman I am because I went through one hell of a time becoming her.

~ Unknown

Malebogo from Botswana, Africa
Photographed by Boingotlo Seitshiro

I Stand
Amazingly Proud

During my heydays as a player on Botswana's National Basketball Team years ago, I met a young man. It was love at first sight. We fell head over heels and we were smitten with one another.

However, over the years our relationship turned sour due to his infidelity and mistrust. We argued constantly. The signs were there in the beginning but I ignored them. He started beating me up and soon it escalated to emotional and mental abuse. Every time we had an argument, he threatened to kill me if I tried to leave him. I was distraught with fear. I kept the battles discreet for fear of exposure to friends and family. The relationship had broken irretrievably and we parted.

Later he came to apologize, asking me to get back with him and work things out. I had already moved on with my life and he would not accept that. He came back again. When I refused again, he was disgruntled.

I was shocked to see him back again on that fateful night. His state of mind was uncompromising and he begged me to open the door. His face changed drastically to that of a monster. He had an evil glint in his grim eyes and I felt terrified. I never saw a real gun in my life and I quivered. I shouted in despair, thinking it would scare him away but within seconds the whole area was filled with an explosion of gunshots. He shot menacingly at the door. It broke into pieces and he forcefully gained entry.

He was standing in front of me, holding the gun, ready to open fire. Who would have thought in a million years that he was capable of such a disheartening and inhumane act? I begged him not to hurt me, not to kill me. He led me out of the house, the cold steel weapon pinned against the side of my face. When he pulled the trigger, a low clicking sound came out. The bullet failed to leave the gun. The gods were with me. It was a defining moment. He loosened his grip on my hand to mend his device. It was my chance to flee for safety.

Bang!

I had not fled much farther when I felt my back instantly shudder. There was a strangely hot and tickling substance piercing through my body, sending hot shivers like an electric drill.

Bang!

The sound came again forcing a surge of energy that charged my senses. It sent me flying and falling face down on the ground. A few more bullets were fired aimlessly at my still body, piercing through fiercely like a double-edged sword. My small frame was consumed with numbness. I did not even feel the hard surface that I landed on. The damage was done — I lay lifelessly. I could not move. Heartless and satisfied, he fired another bullet and he fell to the ground beside me. He committed suicide.

I was battling to breathe. I didn't want to die.

Despite the intense confusion, inwardly, I felt alive. The authorities quickly picked me up from the ground, loaded me into their vehicle and I was rushed to the hospital. I was feeling faint, bleeding profusely and almost lifeless. I was immediately stabilized in the intensive care unit for multiple gunshot wounds.

I had been shot a total of eight times.

I experienced pain and frustration upon learning that one of the bullets had gone through my neck and exited the opposite side of my rib cage causing an extensive amount of damage to my spinal cord. It rendered me a paraplegic. The doctors told me I was terminally injured. There was little chance of survival as the injury was life threatening, and there was no hope of recovery from my condition.

I wallowed in self-pity and thought it would be easier if I had died. But the thought of my mother, her sorrowful face, and the love I felt for her was enough to remind me why I needed to live.

It was a mammoth task to deal with my emotions, my pain, and work my way through the life-challenging situation I faced. Therapy helped me transform and gave me the strength to find inner peace. It helped me to forgive myself for not listening to the signs, to free my heart from hatred, and to forgive him. It was a time when I learned much about courage, acceptance, and forgiveness.

I started channeling my frustrations into something positive. I courageously looked beyond my trauma. I defied all odds by using my devastating experience to motivate, educate, inspire and raise awareness in Botswana about domestic abuse and gender-based violence. I started speaking out on the radio against violence, as well as in workshops and voluntary public forums.

Now I work with various organizations as well as men's groups to come up with problem solving initiatives to eradicate violence against women and girls. I have dedicated my life to teaching young girls about self-esteem and self-respect. I made a significant contribution to help women and children overcome gender oppression and domestic abuse. I taught them about self-love to help them be courageous when undergoing difficulties, and to strive to become courageous under daunting conditions. I also advocate for people with disabilities to help them rehabilitate.

In 2017, in recognition of my selflessness and dedication, I received the International Women of Courage Award from the U.S. Department of State. This prestigious award recognizes women around the globe who have demonstrated exceptional courage and leadership in advocating for peace, justice, human rights, gender equality, and women's empowerment — often at great personal risk.

I also received Botswana's Golden Jubilee Award. I was among 50 phenomenal, inspirational and formidable women, who made a significant difference across the country.

I am a fighter. I am resilient. I am inspirational. I am courageous. I am an example. I have life. No matter what the result is, I stand amazingly proud. Everything else may have changed but I still remain Malebogo Max Molefhe.

Although the world is full of suffering,
it is also full of the overcoming of it.

~ Helen Keller

Anonymous
Photographed by Alisa Divine

A Peaceful Heart & Soul

We were set up on a blind date. He was a farmer and I worked at the office of the United States Department of Agriculture (USDA). Our relationship moved quickly and he asked me to marry him after only three weeks. I was nervous. I put it on hold for three months and we married in a year. It would last for over two decades. He was loving and over-the-top charming — at first.

The abuse didn't happen overnight. It was a slow mind game. It started with his manipulation of the money. Because I got whatever amount he decided, the bills weren't paid if he didn't give me enough money. I only got extra groceries we needed when he was with me. He told me if I ever touched his money (in our joint savings account) he would "break my fucking fingers."

He had relationships with other women. We went to counseling but when a therapist would call him out for his unfaithfulness, he would not go back. We went through several therapists and it always ended quickly. He told me he loved me, that I needed to forgive him and never bring the other women up again. But he really wasn't sorry. To him, the pain I was going through didn't matter. When I cried over him being with other women, he would use both of his feet to shove me off the bed and tell me to lie on the floor. I told my mom and sister about the other women and that was when I broke down. But I kept most of the abuse hidden.

He was not mean all of the time and that's one reason why I didn't leave earlier. Sometimes he would be really nice and affectionate. He was loving with the kids. I think he liked being married to me so he could portray an image of a good, family man. I helped make that happen because I wanted a normal, healthy family and I worked very hard at it. I also felt I had to save him from his demons. My marriage was like a house of cards though. It was fragile, like a vase and I had to polish it.

However, when the kids started school, I started to change. I volunteered and began to notice the difference between my world and the world of other women. They were not the same. My husband was no longer a husband in my eyes. I realized it didn't matter if I looked perfect or if I was the best lover. I could never be whatever it was he was seeking.

During the last five years of our marriage, the physical and sexual abuse heightened. He tried to strangle me. He described to me how easily he could snap my neck. He said he wanted to know what it would feel like to kill someone. He sodomized me. The first time he cried and told me he was sorry he caused me so much pain. He said he couldn't help himself — he was so turned on by me. The times after that he didn't feel bad at all, even though I begged him to stop and told him that it hurt me so badly for days. He believed I was his property to do with what he wanted. I still loved him but I began not liking him.

When he broke my nose, I went to the hospital, and the state police were called in. The female officer questioned me in ways where I couldn't cover for him any longer. It was the first time I shared all of the details. The escalation during those last few weeks was drastic. I wanted to get him help. I told the police I didn't want to press charges. But the officer told me the case was between my husband and the state —a man cannot hurt his wife. They filed more than a handful of charges against him; domestic violence, criminal sexual conduct and attempted murder.

People were shocked when they found out that he had hurt me.

I always took pride in telling the truth, even he said that many times. The more I've thought about it, I wasn't telling the truth. I didn't tell anyone about the abuse. I portrayed to my kids and my family that everything was okay. They didn't realize how he was treating me behind closed doors.

We went to counseling through the courts and he even verbally abused me during a counseling session. That was when he showed he had no remorse. He changed his story and maintained the facade that he didn't hurt me. With advisement, I filed for divorce nearly one year after he broke my nose.

I was assigned an advocate after filing for divorce and she began giving me information about abuse. At first I didn't want to hear it. Then I started to listen. It's hard to explain to others because he was my world. It was important to me that my family stay together. And my world was making sure he was seen as a good man. He could be a good man after all, sometimes, and that is what I clung to for so long.

I continued counseling and walked through many things that were difficult. One was to stop carrying the blame for the damage that occurred in our family.

Another was to learn there was another world beyond my abusive marriage. My youngest son and I moved when he was a senior in high school, to create a fresh start. I took on several jobs with determination to make it on my own. I started thinking differently. I wanted to be independent.

I chose to go back to school and obtain an esthetician license. It was a journey going to school with young people when I was 50. I now work at a medical spa with people who care for each other and work together as a team. I feel I relate to a lot of people coming in and I can understand their skincare concerns. I love working with them and developing relationships.

I moved in the right direction. I finally have peace. And it's not because he stopped behaving in ways I feel angry over — but because I realized it's ok to put up a boundary to protect myself. I don't have to give up myself, ever again. I cut off all contact with him because I know he would attempt to manipulate me as he did in the past and I no longer accept that. I know I can have a healthy relationship because I'm in one now with someone who listens to me without judgment. My kids and I are very close. They are good people and I feel fortunate we all are happy and thriving.

Two roads diverged in a wood
and I took the one less traveled by,
and that has made all the difference.

~Robert Frost

Linda from Georgia
Photographed by Leticia Andrade

Never Looking Back

My ex-husband called off our wedding three weeks before the date. I had already paid for my dress, my parents had already paid for a hall, and the invitations were already in the mail. We married later but without a formal wedding reception. At our wedding, he had a broken hand. He got it by attempting to hit me but he missed. He hit the wall of the elevator where we were instead. I know at this point you might be asking why did I still marry him? The answer was simple. I thought I was in love. I also was very young — I had just turned 20. I still have the wedding photo of me in a tunic dress that I bought off the rack and he in a suit with a cast on his hand.

He was abusive from the start and it only got worse as time went on. There was one incident when I was in the bathtub and he held a hair dryer over the tub threatening, "All I would need to do is drop this in the tub right now and you would be gone."

On another occasion, he knocked me down and my backside hit the concrete floor so hard I could not move. When he told me to get up and I didn't, it enraged him further so he started kicking me. I recall not being able to sit or lay back in a bathtub for many years afterwards.

When I finally had enough I just knew it. I had to find a way to get out. He never allowed me to work, so I knew that moving on would be hard. But it happened. He came home from work one day and asked me if I had paid the bills with the money he had left me. I told him I did and the receipts were right there on the counter next to him. He quickly looked at the counter and started yelling at me to get up and come over and show them to him.

I knew in my heart that was not going to end well. But I was not going to give in to him. Again I repeated that the receipts were right on the counter by the phone where he was standing. In a rage he came over to me, pulled the rocking chair with me in it over to the counter and slammed my head on the counter. He asked me again and again. I said to myself this is it...and I replied, "NO, they are right there in front you." I was determined. I just knew that was going to be it and I might not live beyond that day. He knocked over a nearby six-foot glass-shelving unit and then went into the bedroom. I went over and sat on the sofa, knowing my two young girls were across the street at the playground.

I just waited and then I heard the BANG – I could not move. I could smell the smoke! I started thinking OMG he killed himself. But then again, he loved himself way too much to do that. At that moment he started walking down the hallway towards me with the gun in his hand and waving it up and down. He was saying, "Look what you made me do – Look what you made me do!" I rose so very slowly and tried to maneuver to the front door so I could get away. I cautiously walked around the big coffee table and managed to get outside. I ran around the corner to my neighbor's house, so frightened I could not even speak. I might have been in shock. After about 15 minutes I returned to the house to make sure the girls were ok. I looked in the bedroom and the small TV that he shot was gone. When the girls came home and saw the mess in the house I sent them to another neighbor's house to keep them safe.

Later that evening he came back home and I asked him what he did with the TV. "What TV? I don't see a TV," he said. The next morning I asked him to leave and he agreed. The girls and I stayed at the house but we had to sell it quickly so he could get half of the money. I began to move on with my life by finding an apartment, a job, and taking care of the girls. My dad co-signed for me on a car and my parents babysat once a week so I could spend time with my friends. Some of them were going through a divorce also. They became my therapy. We have remained close to this day, even though we live in different states.

As I expected, my ex didn't make it easy on us. The child support payments rarely ever arrived. He called to say he would pick up the girls and then not show up, leaving them waiting for hours. To this day at mutual family gatherings, I find it very difficult to be in proximity of him after almost 40 years. His violent patterns continue. The police have been called on domestic violence reports from his second wife too.

My story has a happy ending.

During the times I spent with my girlfriends, I met the love of my life and we have been married for 35 years. I thank God everyday for my

115

husband who has always stood with me through all of the craziness. He has helped me raise two beautiful women. We also share a great son-in-law and three fantastic grandchildren.

As best friends, we are moving on to the next stage of our lives. We plan to grow old together, travel the world and never look back.

The secret of change is to focus all of your energy,
not on fighting the old, but on building the new.

~ Socrates

Lawful Decisions

As a deputy law enforcement officer, I was a woman unlikely to be characterized as a victim of domestic abuse. I was expected to be strong, powerful, and not take crap from anyone. By sharing my story, I want others to realize that domestic violence is inclusive of all demographics — every race, religion, age, occupation, income level, and education level.

I was a young mom, with two little girls when I met my abuser. He was extremely charming, handsome, and persistent. After we married, things began to subtly change. Something in my gut told me our relationship wasn't real. He brought me gifts to work, but only to check up on me.

If I mentioned anything about separation or divorce, he threatened suicide. Often. If he stormed out of the house after an argument, he would call me from the middle of the train tracks saying he would let the train run over him because I didn't love him or want to make it work. I couldn't tell anyone. I was a law enforcement officer. If this was happening in my own home, how could I possibly maintain my career? I felt trapped.

It escalated from there. He accused me of sleeping with co-workers if I came home late. He continued to show up with gifts at work. Everyone thought it was "nice" except for one friend, another deputy. She pulled me aside one day and confronted me. "I see what he's doing, he's constantly calling and paging you, showing up to check on you." I started crying and divulged more details. She said, "Doris - that's abuse." I argued with her. I said he wasn't hitting me or physically hurting me. She started to tell me about domestic violence. She was the one to help me see.

The same deputy was visiting me when my abuser called. I told him we were done. He threatened to burn our house down. My friend heard it and called the police. I was horrified others would know. He was arrested for harassment and went to jail. I attempted to get a permanent restraining order and it was denied. The magistrate said, "Honey, I don't think you are in an abusive relationship. This seems like a female thing. You need to work on some things in your marriage." That heightened my humiliation.

I finally made the decision that my marriage was over when my 10-year-old daughter came to me in tears. "Mom I know you guys argue all the time, I hear you fighting. I'm afraid he's going to hurt you. Sometimes I don't fall asleep at night because I wait next to the door so I can call the police if he tries to hurt you." I thanked her for being brave and confiding in me. I didn't want my daughters to think that abuse is acceptable.

Immediately I put a safety plan together with an advocate from TESSA. I changed the locks on the doors. I changed bank accounts. I included my mom in the safety plan. She knew what to do if I wasn't home at the expected time. I changed routes to and from work daily. When he began to stalk me, I filed a restraining order, and this time a male magistrate granted it.

I heard nothing from him for a week until I came home from an evening shift at work. I was on light duty, while nursing an ankle sprain. I wasn't in uniform, nor did I have my gun on me. As I walked up my driveway I noticed a dark silhouette coming towards me. He had been hiding under the steps nearby. He grabbed my arm and demanded me to go with him.

> *He showed me the gun he had.*
> *A million thoughts went through my mind. Do I fight him?*
> *If I lose the fight, does he kill me?*
> *Does he then go inside and kill my family?*

I went with him to take the fight elsewhere. He forced me to take off all my clothes and to perform oral sex on him while he was driving. I thought about jumping out of his truck but I had a sprained ankle. He had a gun. He was an ex-marine. He took me to a deserted train track where he raped me. I froze. I reverted to the little girl I once was and I cried. I couldn't fight, I couldn't scream, I just let him do what he did. I had to go to the bathroom and he let me put one leg out of the truck to urinate. I wiped myself with the Taco Bell napkins from the truck to leave evidence on the ground pointing to him — in case he killed me.

In the meantime, my phone was going off constantly. He became scared and panicked trying to decide what to do next. I asked him to take me home and I would not tell anyone what happened. I convinced him that things would work out.

When we started to leave, I asked to get something to eat and he noticed a convenience store. He made me go in with him. I asked to use the bathroom — after he inspected it to ensure there was no escape route. I turned the faucet on. I cried. I threw up. And then I started praying. I was desperate. I needed to be saved. My girls needed me. I made a promise to God that if he saved me, I would make it my life's mission to make a difference in this world. A feeling of peace and love washed over me for the first time. I knew I was going to be ok. I turned the faucet off and I composed myself. He had bought me a candy bar and a purple bottle of Propel to drink. We were in the truck and when I took a bite I thought I would throw up again. I asked him for unflavored water. He insisted I go back in with him but I told him I couldn't, I would pass out.

Throughout the kidnapping, he was extremely meticulous. But then he made one mistake he will probably regret for the rest of his life.

He left the key in the ignition.

As soon as he went into the store, I jumped into the driver's seat and put it in reverse. I saw him turn around. The look on his face was priceless.

I got onto the highway on the wrong side of the road and was driving like a maniac. And still I felt safe. I honked my horn, flashed my lights and drove 100 mph.

When I approached my neighborhood, I saw the flashing lights. I turned the corner and the police cars were there. I stopped and they had weapons pointed at me. I got out with my hands in the air. "It's Doris!" my fellow officers yelled. A deputy ran over to me and I collapsed. They comforted me and then got the information they needed. They searched for him all night and didn't find him until the next day, hiding at his father's house inside the kitchen cupboards, like a coward. He's been locked up ever since. He was convicted and got life in prison.

I eventually addressed my brokenness. I went to counseling and found a church community that embraced me. I learned to release the anger, the bitterness and to forgive, in order to move on with my life. I met an amazing man who was supportive and patient enough to allow me to work through things and learn to trust again. We've been married for 10 years and he's been a blessing in my life. We have a son together.

*I have turned around the evil that existed in my life —
not just to survive but to thrive and live truly free.*

In 2007, I was on *Oprah* to tell my story as a woman in law enforcement and a victim of domestic violence. I have become a leader by speaking to church organizations and the law enforcement community on how to recognize domestic violence and what steps need to be improved. I speak at the local and national levels, and in the media. I had a two-part session on *Focus on the Family* with host Jim Daly. In addition, I am on the board of Break The Silence of Domestic Violence.

Most importantly, I want others to know that domestic violence is not a private matter — everyone should make it their business. Others will thank you, like I thanked my fellow deputy friend who stepped into my life.

If you can't fly, then run, if you can't run, then walk, if you can't walk, then crawl, but whatever you do, you have to keep moving forward.

~ Martin Luther King

Leslie from Washington, District of Columbia
Photographed by Alisa Divine

CRAZY LOVE CONFESSIONS

I grew up in a family that looked perfect. My father was a lawyer. My mother was a teacher. Our house sat on a leafy green street at the top of a hill.

Nearly everyone in my family went to Harvard.

We were all blonde.

Behind closed doors, my mother drank too much, too often. My father, the first in his family to finish high school, turned to workaholism and the outward trappings of success. Even on weekends, he was rarely home.

A year after graduating from Harvard myself, while working at my first job at *Seventeen* magazine in New York City, I met a handsome man on the subway. He too had just graduated from an Ivy League university. He worked at an impressive Wall Street bank. I felt sorry for him when he confided that his stepfather abused him as a child. My parents had just gotten divorced. I was desperate for family. I fell in love with him like falling off a cliff.

Five days before our wedding, this man strangled me. I had never imagined any man would ever hurt me. I couldn't get past my disbelief that the one I loved more than all the others wanted to destroy me. Over the next two years, he held a Colt .45 revolver to my head, threw my food on the floor and pulled the keys out of the car ignition as I drove down the highway. I refused to admit I was a battered wife. I was a strong, smart woman in love with a troubled man — until the December night when he beat me badly enough that I realized he would kill me if I stayed. The time had come to choose him or me.

I chose me.

My mother gave me money but no one else in my family knew how to help. Friends and strangers, including two policemen, a domestic violence advocate, a lawyer, a therapist and a locksmith showed me how I might turn the end of my marriage into a new life.

Some family members didn't understand why I left my husband. Including my father.

Five years later, I remarried a stable, grounded man. He met my two most important criteria: he wasn't an alcoholic and he wasn't abusive. I got pregnant. We moved to a new city. We had a normal life. I wrote a book about my first marriage. I was happy-ish, and that felt like more than enough after what I'd been through.

Eventually, I divorced my second husband for the same reasons I married him: he was so unemotional that living with him felt like psychological abuse. My standards for the men in my life had gotten unimaginably higher than the day I married him.

The three beautiful children we created together are thriving as adults. The only guns they knew as kids were plastic water pistols. Together, my kids and I broke my family's cycle of alcoholism and abuse.

My mother died from cancer in my home at age 75. It was a privilege to care for her as she declined, despite our problems. I was the one who discovered her in our guest bed the morning after she died. That moment was as priceless to me as the day each of my children were born.

I haven't spoken with my father in ten years, and the silence between us feels like one of the greatest gifts I have given myself.

I am in my 50s now. Almost three decades have passed since I left my abusive first husband. My life doesn't look perfect from here. Alcoholism. Relationship violence. Two ex-husbands. Family members who don't talk to each other.

> *Sometimes I imagine my parallel life,*
> *the one I would be living if I hadn't left*
> *the damaged men in my life.*
> *Where would I be if people hadn't helped me*
> *and I hadn't helped myself?*
> *My life today is crowded with family, books,*
> *men who love me, friends, animals and joy.*

A treasured friend once said she thought I had been terribly unlucky in life. A small voice inside responded, Life is not what happens to you. It's what you make of what happens to you.

Seeing life that way, I have always been lucky. It's not where you come from or how often you fail that matters. It's where you end up.

Leslie Morgan Steiner is a domestic violence prevention advocate and the author of the *New York Times* bestselling memoir, *Crazy Love*. Her *TEDTalk* on why domestic violence victims stay in abusive relationships has been viewed by more than four million people in 41 countries.

She found herself over a long and treacherous road and the more treacherous the road became, the more of her she found.

~ Atticus

Kathryn from California
Photographed by Neon Howe

HOPE

My story begins when I was a young woman. Growing up, I was the person that people would overlook. I never had a boyfriend. I was a chubby adolescent. So when my future husband and I were teenagers, he showed me the love and attention that was missing in my life. I thought I found love. We had a great relationship in the early stages, great enough for us to want to get married. I was creating the love I wanted and then we began having babies.

Slowly, from then on, things started to change. My husband began to become paranoid about everything I did. He wanted complete control over me. Accusations of me cheating on him with neighbors, his brother, whomever he could think of, caused him to keep me locked up in the house. I never even thought of doing any of the things he accused me of. But this didn't go on all the time. He praised me often and treated me well. Then a cycle of violence took over with hitting and verbal abuse.

I never quite understood his behavior. I just wished he'd return to the person that I fell in love with. Being married and in love with him, I felt we had an obligation to try and work the marriage out. I wanted to be a good wife and mother. I thought it was my responsibility to fix my family, if not for us, at least for our children. We tried counseling, however I was always too afraid of the consequences if I told the truth and so I never did. He threatened to kill my children and me if I left. So I lied in counseling, saying that everything was just fine.

Everything was not fine. I remember times when he would have me sit in a chair, then walk around me and say mean, cruel things. He told me I was stupid, called me a "whore" and told me I could never do anything on my own. All the while in my own mind, I was countering what he was saying, because I knew I was more than what he told me. I did not know how to get out of the situation. Not by myself, especially having three children.

The transition occurred when we were in a hotel in Barstow, California. His fury peaked for whatever reason and I found myself on the floor, with his hands around my neck. I felt powerless. Of all the times he had been violent, that time, I knew he was going to kill me. Feeling that certainty of death, I had to fight back. I managed to get him off me and incapacitated long enough for me to get out and get help!

I made my way into a shelter, protected, while he searched as hard as he could to find the children and me.

My sister-in-law and mother were responsible for hiding my children until the time that they could join me at the shelter. He threatened to hurt my family and hurt himself, if they didn't get me back to him. Fortunately, no one gave out any information to him. Time passed. I spent two days in one shelter, a week in another until I finally ended up in Modesto at the Women's Haven Center, where I would learn the skills needed to make it without him. It was not easy, but that shelter was my gateway and eventually I learned to come into my own power. It was more than just getting away — I needed to stay away for good. I began to realize that I was more than the horrible things he used to call me. I realized the shift one day when he visited our children and he started in on me with accusations again. But I knew I was a good woman and good mother. I no longer tried to convince him otherwise or even care what he thought. Instead, I told him to get out and I never looked back.

After 10 years of abuse, I now live a happier life with a new husband that respects and loves me for the person that I am. I am the Public Works Director for the City of Newman. My family supports the Haven Center with donations and appearances. My children have grown into smart, productive members of society, and are all college graduates. My daughter was 7 years old when we were at the Haven Center and today she is on the Board of Directors there. It is a full circle of love.

My wish in sharing my story is to give others hope and strength to know that there is help available if they are in a domestic abuse environment. They need to know that they are not alone and they will never be alone. They need to seek a shelter or find a mentor in order to get the help they and their family deserves.

Truly powerful women don't explain why they want respect.
They simply don't engage those
who don't give it to them.

~ Unknown

Conclusion

The year was 1988. I was 11 years old and I flew for the first time — even solo. I was given the opportunity to spend a week with my aunt who lived in Chicago. The plan was for my Uncle to drive me to Chicago from my home in Michigan and I would fly home the following week. In the weeks leading up to my trip, I began to feel anxious about flying. I had recently watched *Hostage Flight* (1985 TV movie) about a Trans Allied flight that was hijacked by terrorists. The passengers on the plane plotted together and fought back. In the time leading up to my first flight, I had a feeling I needed to prepare myself for the possibility of a hijacking.

In my head, I rehearsed and memorized a script. I knew I would be brave. I knew I would stand up on the plane once the hijackers presented themselves and I would shout, "You can't do this, it isn't right! You can't hurt these people!" I thought my words could make a difference. My 11-year-old self was prepared and I felt certain I would be called to step up.

The week soared by and soon it was time for my flight home. Aunt Donna escorted me to the gate in O'Hare International Airport and left me in the care of a flight attendant who made sure I found my seat and felt comfortable. I sat quietly thinking about my mother waiting to hug me at the small airport in Michigan. I thought about my script. I had silently rehearsed it all week while in Chicago. I felt anxious and yet, ready.

Much to my relief, however, my flight was free of any malicious activity and I actually sat next to a businesswoman who offered to share her box of high-end chocolates with me.

The experience sharpened my perception. I can say in retrospect, it was a foreshadowing. It was an awakening I felt within my soul that I was going to be called to stand up for something larger than me. I felt I had some sort of purpose — standing up for others, with others. I felt brave surrounding myself with people who were willing to be brave with me.

Over the next thirty years of my life, between 1988 and 2018, there were many twists and turns. I underwent rigorous qualification for my calling to step up, even though I wasn't aware that it was taking place. It was not terrorism I became qualified in, but domestic abuse. I was in an abusive relationship that ran a course of 18 years. After several attempts throughout those years, I was able to free myself and move beyond it.

That background, along with several additional factors, led me to create something bigger than the pain I felt. I became a writer, a photographer, a business owner, and co-owner of a publishing company, Personal Power Press. I discovered the more I created, the smaller and smaller the pain became. It led me to find women who wanted to tell their stories and turn their pain into power. It led me to this book, to what I feel is my purpose, my calling to step up. It led me to join a force of bravery with my sisters and proclaim that our spirits would not stay crushed. It led me to now — to stand up, not on a hijacked plane, but to shout to the men everywhere who have been abusive, "You can't do this, it isn't right! You cannot hurt these women!"

Through the creation of this piece of art, I have uncovered the best version of myself. I believe my words can make a difference. I want others to know, that they too can overcome even the worst of situations and go on to lead lives full of meaning and purpose. Despite my rigorous and often agonizing qualification process, I have turned my pain into my power. This book you now hold in your hands is proof of that. I feel the empowerment and it is my mission to capture the irrepressible spirit of domestic abuse survivors through stories and photographs.

The time has come for all of us to join forces. There is a cataclysmic shift happening in our society and women are speaking up and speaking out. They are demanding that change occur. They are demanding respect and equality.

What I ask of you — whether you are male or female, young or old, abused or not — is to reach out to support your sisters around the world in raising their voices and staying strong. Encourage them to speak up, speak out, and get the help they need.

They too, can turn their pain into power.

Now — my moment has arrived. I am qualified and I am ready to stand up to the challenge.

I am proud of the woman I have become. *#SheWins*

Alisa Divine

About the Photographers

Neon Howe is a portrait photographer based in Modesto, California. He is self-taught, but holds a degree in Computer Science from San Diego State University.

Through his love of art and people, Neon aims to use his photography as a way to help reflect back to people the beauty he sees in them as well as help raise awareness for the different causes he likes to champion. Topics surrounding empowering women, poverty, and homelessness are just a few that are dear to his heart. When not photographing, he enjoys spending time with his family, and adventuring where life takes them.

Neon Howe
Modesto, California
www.neonhowe.com
hello@neonhowe.com
@neonhoweportraits
209-560-0876

Karianne Munstedt is a portrait photographer in Phoenix, Arizona. She is an artist and nurturer, fiercely motivated by using her talents to make women feel confident, empowered, and whole. Growing up with an abusive role model left her filled with fear. She countered this by attempting to be perfect, but never took the time to understand who she was. She continued down a path of perfection that led her to a marriage, a job, and other endeavors that weren't right for her.

Karianne started a journey to get to know herself in her 30s. On her spiritual journey, she connected back to the thing that brought her joy as a child… photography. She discovered an innate talent to capture a person's true inner beauty. In 2018, she left her full-time corporate job to focus on what brings her joy… her portrait business.

Personally, Karianne is a wife, doggy momma, stepmother, and new mommy to an infant son.

Karianne Munstedt
Phoenix, Arizona
www.kariannemunstedt.com
kari@kariannemunstedt.com
@KarianneMunstedtPortrait
623-341-5745

Leticia Andrade is a portrait photographer based in Peachtree City, Georgia. She was born and raised in the mountains outside of Rio de Janeiro, Brazil, where she lived until the early 1990s. At the age of 20, Leticia moved to the U.S. where she studied Art History at Syracuse University and developed a career in the fashion design industry. After 10 years caring for her two children, Leticia felt it was time to do something that would reignite her passion for the arts and creativity.

In 2016, Leticia Andrade Photography was born. Today her studio invites women of all ages and walks of life, to celebrate the power and beauty throughout the portrait process. Her purpose to help women improve confidence and self-value is clearly revealed in her work. In a safe place, free of judgment, Leticia's ability to connect with her subjects empowers them to be authentic and experience a session that will change the way they see themselves forever.

Leticia Andrade
Peachtree City, Georgia
www.lehphoto.com
leticiaandrade@lehphoto.com
@lehphoto
470-255-0095

Michelle Taylor Jones has had a love affair with all things beautiful since high school. She practiced putting makeup on her friends and followed with taking their pictures. She felt a fire burning in her soul. Throughout the last 18 years, she has perfected how to pose and shape each of her clients with various body shapes. Michelle has created her own style of boudoir that is tasteful and focuses on each woman's inner beauty with lingerie as a smaller detail. She is proud that she creates timeless images for her clients that mirror their beauty back to them.

Michelle's career excelled when she met Sue Bryce in 2015 and began adding contemporary portraiture to her photo sessions. She went on to open a second level of her studio in 2017, and added a full-time hair salon as well. She has never looked back and continues to push herself to dream bigger.

Michelle Taylor Jones
Snohomish, Washington
www.michelletaylorportraits.com
info@michelletaylorportraits.com
@michelletaylorportraits
206-678-3718

For the last decade, **Alisa Divine** has been supporting women to develop a powerful self-image, through her portraiture. After apprenticing with world-class photographers, she began photographing high school senior girls and later women of all ages. Her goal was to help them feel confident and empowered as they transitioned to a new stage in life.

As a result of the profound effects she saw from working with high school senior girls, Alisa was inspired to create the *More Than Beautiful Project*™. This program expanded beyond photography, to include six months of life coaching for young women. She coaches them to develop healthy body images, identify their voices, step out as leaders, and become the woman they want to be.

Through the publishing company she co-owns, Personal Power Press, Alisa has produced two books raising awareness about the issue of domestic violence, *#SheWins* and *Killing Kate*.

Alisa Divine
Frankenmuth, Michigan
www.alisadivine.com
info@alisadivine.com
@divine_images

Photographer **Boingotlo Karabo Seitshiro** is from Gaborone, Botswana. She was a young female photographer when she started her journey in 2013, using a Nikon D5100, a 15-55 and a 70-300 Sigma lens, which she still currently uses. She is also a graduate of Journalism from Limkokwing University. As a female photographer, she chose not to be discouraged in a male-dominated industry. She learned new techniques and improved her work by going through YouTube tutorials and researching the ways veteran photographers create a million dollar photograph. She also goes through old work to see where she can improve. For her, photography is an enhanced version of life, where reality is captured for one to observe each detail of moments lived. She feels excited when traveling and photographing new scenery and also taking black and white artistic photographs which capture the depth and soul of a subject.

Boingotlo Seitshiro
Botswana, Africa
www.boiiksphotography.co.bw/#home
boiseitshiro@gmail.com
@BoiiKSPhotography
+267-7518-2170

Mellissa Baker is an accredited photographer from Perth, Australia where she lives with her hubby and their two sons. She loves to create, to teach and loves to support and inspire other women.

Her business is called Steering the Mothership - A place where photography & motherhood come together. She specializes in outdoor and in-home lifestyle photo sessions for families and offers an online camera & photography course. She also runs a project that is a portrait and story collection of women navigating through the highs and lows of their motherhood journey. Information about her photo sessions, camera course and motherhood project can be found on her website.

Mellissa Baker
Perth, Australia
www.steeringthemothership.com
steeringthemothership@gmail.com
@steeringthemothership

Mikey is a freelance photographer. As a teenager he has always been fond of imagery and lighting. The way light dances is so intriguing. Entwining that with peoples' stories, just made sense. With a drive to unfold broken times into beautiful chapters of a journey called life, he believes capturing these moments is vital to the heart.

You can email him at climb4recovery@gmail.com
"Remember... capture everything."

Michael Oliver
Boston, Massachusetts
climb4recovery@gmail.com
@nextchaptercreatives

Starting **Rachel Thompson-Moore** Photography was a dream come true for her. She loves giving her clients the memories that they can cherish forever. From documenting the love story of a young couple getting married, to capturing the sweet moments of a newborn's first days of life, to chasing little ones around, to giving a senior a great experience during her last year in high school — she wants to tell the story of her clients with photos.

When she is not capturing memories for her clients, you can find her surrounded by her four boys (3 kids, 1 husband) at either a baseball or football field cheering for them. She lives for girl's night out with the same friends she has had since high school. Sleeping in is only a dream.

Rachel Thompson-Moore
Greeneville, South Carolina
www.rtmphotosc.com
rachel@rtmphotosc.com
@rachelthompsonmoorephoto
843-241-0410

Regina Perry, aka Reggie, is a self-taught amateur photographer based out of Falmouth, MA but serving all of New England. What started out as a hobby, a way to capture all of the beauty in this world and hold on to it forever, soon began turning into a business opportunity. She then started her own business, Rising Roots Photography. Recently, Reggie has had a number of photos published in local magazines, one of them being the cover of a yearly publication.

When Reggie isn't talking in third person and awkwardly sharing facts about herself, she likes to spend time with her 6, yep - SIX! children. They all enjoy adventuring in the woods, swimming in the ocean, road trips, eating food, random dance parties, snuggling, and laughing. Regina is also a survivor of domestic violence. #**SheWins**

Regina Perry
Falmouth, Massachusetts
risingrootsphotography@gmail.com
@RisingRootsPhotography
901-497-4854

Special Thanks

Thomas Haller, this book exists because of you. This is a full circle. You are the "Morrie to my Tuesdays." Thank you for having my back. The best way I know to express my gratitude is to take what you have taught me and pass it on to others. Personal Power Press is going to be busy.

Sue Bryce, in November of 2015, in Los Angeles, you told me to turn my weakness into my greatest strength. Here it is. You have been an inspiration to me in many ways. Most of all, thank you for being an example of an empowered woman.

Melissa McFarlane, thank you for helping me to approach this book in a new way. Thank you for believing in me and also teaching me to believe. You've played a significant role in this.

Mary Sue Barry, thank you for helping me discover this path. Then, as you so eloquently put it, "stepped out." You were a messenger, a guide to show me the way.

Joan Ramm, little did we know, when I was a student in your college English class that 20+ years later, I would produce this book and you would edit it. Thank you for sharing your expertise and joining me in this experience. Thanks for introducing me to **Val Walderzak** — you both stepped in and took me under your wings.

Chris Zehnder, you are the anchor so I can be the wings — thank you. I appreciate your respect, your unwavering loyalty, and the freedom to soar. I love you with all of my heart, everyday more and more. With you and the family we have created is where I want to be.

About the Author

Alisa Divine is co-owner and Vice President of Personal Power Press, a publishing company that provides a platform for others to share their stories of turning pain into power. She is a Life Coach for young women, helping them transition from where they are to where they want to be. Alisa also has founded, *The More Than Beautiful Project*™, which is a program for teenage girls to build confidence, develop a positive body image, and learn key components of healthy relationships. She is on the Board of Directors for the Saginaw County Underground Railroad, serving survivors of domestic violence in Mid-Michigan.

Alisa's mission is to empower women who have survived domestic violence as well as empower teenage girls to become the best version of themselves at an early age. She feels a great purpose to encourage others to rise above their circumstances and triumph.

Alisa lives in Michigan with her husband, and their blended family with eight children.

Visit the #SheWins online community at:
www.Facebook.com/SheWinsBook/

I am beneath or above no one.
When I am independent of the good or bad opinion of others,
I stand strong in my own divine power.

~ Deepak Chopra